HOW TO LEGALLY **REDUCE YOUR TAX** WITHOUT LOSING ANY MONEY

Discover how the rich use company and trust structures to protect their assets and minimise their tax.

ED CHAN

www.chan-naylor.com.au

How to Legally Reduce Your Tax

Published by
CNIP Pty Ltd
Suite 5, Level 2, 55 Grandview Street Pymble
NSW 2073, Australia
Phone 02 9391 5000
www.chan-naylor.com.au
First Printed 2005
This edition published in 2018

National Library of Australia Cataloguing-in-Publication entry

Author:	1973- Ed Chan.
Title:	How to legally reduce your tax / Ed Chan.
ISBN:	978-0-6482583-0-8 (pbk.)
Subjects:	Tax incidence—Australia. Tax planning—Australia.
	Trusts and trustees—Taxation—Australia.
	Asset–liability management—Taxation—Australia.
	Real estate investment—Taxation—Australia.
	Estate planning—Taxation—Australia.
Other Authors/	
Contributors:	Chan, Edward Sai-Ping, 1959-
Dewey Number:	336.2940994

Typeset by Working Type Studio — www.workingtype.com.au

About the Author

Ed Chan

Edward Chan was born in Papua New Guinea in 1959. He completed his secondary and tertiary education in Sydney before becoming a Certified Practising Accountant. He began his career in the early 1980s, working with PKF International and various other practices, and in 1984 he began his own practice, called Chan & Naylor.

Today Ed is the Chairman of Chan & Naylor Business, Property and Tax Accountants, which is recognised within the profession as being one of Australia's leading accountancy firms. It specialises in small businesses, self-managed superannuation funds and structuring of property investments. Chan & Naylor is the model firm studied by thousands of students when completing their CPA program with the Australian Society of Certified Accountants. Chan & Naylor is also studied by students completing their MBA at Queensland University. Chan & Naylor won BRW's Fastest Growing Accountancy Firm for 3 years running and is ranked 37th in the top 100 Accountancy Firms in Australia.

Ed is a seasoned and passionate property investor and developer. His unique understanding of the relationship between property investment and tax makes him one of only few accountants who truly understand how to structure investments for asset protection and tax minimisation.

ALSO BY ED CHAN:

How to Achieve Wealth for Life

How to Buy Property with Your Super Money

Small to Great

He has been a regular presenter at property investment and professional seminars held by the Institute of Chartered Accountants in Australia and the Institute of Public Accountants.

Ed Chan has had a profound impact on the way the entire accountancy profession operates, through the development of compliance systems and practices. He is a director of EknowHowAccounting Pty Ltd, which has a membership of over 520 accountancy firms around Australia that subscribe to the company's unique system of operations. He is also a regular presenter on best-practice methodologies to over 4000 accountants in public practice around Australia.

Ed lives with his wife and three children in Sydney.

Ed's Dedication

To my wife, Donna, and children Amy, Ryan and Mitchell.
You are the barometer of my success.
I feel extremely successful and lucky to have you.

Disclaimer

The material in this publication is of a general nature, and neither purports nor intends to be advice. Readers should not act on the basis of any matter in this publication without taking professional advice from a licensed Financial Planner, with due regard to their own particular circumstances. The authors and publisher expressly disclaim all and any liability to any person, whether a purchaser of this publication or not, in respect of anything and of the consequences of anything done or omitted to be done by any such person in reliance, whether whole or partial, upon the whole or any part of the contents of this publication.

Contents

Introduction

This book is simple.

While the title of this book is "How to legally reduce your tax",[1] its scope and objectives are more far- reaching.

Its purpose is to make you a "Player".

Having studied accountancy and been involved in business for many years, we have realised one thing— people tend to overcomplicate things and tax is no exception. The law is *always* changing. Believe it or not, percentages, tax rulings[2] and what you can and cannot do change, almost daily! However, while these things are important, what is more important is that you first grasp the basic fundamentals which allow for an understanding of the more complex aspects of tax, and thankfully these fundamentals don't change (much!).

Broad ignorance of these fundamentals is evident by the number of schemes[3] we have witnessed over the years—schemes which advocate

1 **tax**: the charge against a person, their property or an activity for the support of the government.

2 **ruling**: decision by authority: an official or binding decision such as one made by a court or judge.

3 "Schemes" in this context relates to aggressive methods of avoiding tax which usually end up being exposed and rejected by the ATO (and by aggressive we mean characterised by a willingness to accept above-average risk in pursuit of above-average returns). The penalty for those involved in such schemes can range from fines to a jail term. Tax reduction is obviously a popular subject as tax affects all of us who work and earn money. Many people, in an effort to reduce their tax burden, have sought ways to minimise tax. Due no doubt to the complexity of tax laws and the lack of tax education provided to the everyday Australian, ignorance has led them to employ aggressive tax schemes recommended by those "in the know". No such schemes are advocated by the authors; our purpose lies in providing understanding and thus application of sensible and workable methods. The authors and their educational materials, seminars and workshops do not promote or condone aggressive schemes. For more information on aggressive tax planning the reader is advised to visit https://www.ato.gov.au/General/Tax-planning/

tax benefits. Some of these schemes require the participant to invest money and suffer a loss in the hope of long-term gain. The "great" reward is a tax deduction on the loss. Other schemes require the setting up of numerous different structures to flick money here and there. Both types of scheme are unnecessary.

Why is it that so many people are led to believe that losing or spending money is the only means of saving tax? The fact is: there is no easy way for an individual to find out how the system really works. Fundamental tax laws are not taught in schools. No curriculum has been developed for the everyday worker who is eager to learn how the game is played.

No matter what you are earning right now, or where you lie in the "classes", it *is* possible for you to enjoy the tax benefits the rich have been using for many years. This book is the start of your educational process and your first step into the realm of the "Player", which is someone who knows how to play the game of tax and win!

You see, we believe that:

1. Every Australian has the right to learn how the system works.
2. Every Australian has the right to services that help them implement what they have learned.
3. The most effective knowledge is that which can be understood and applied.

That is why we have designed an educational process in the form of books, DVDs, and events that are 1) simple, affordable and 3) accessible for everyone who wants to learn more.

You'll find that this book is broken up into three parts. Part 1 covers the game rules; this is where you learn the basics of the game called tax and how to keep score. Part 2 introduces some of the tools you can use, including structures like companies and trusts. And lastly, Part 3 contains real life examples of how the game is played using some of the tools you will have learned about.

To aid in understanding, this book contains a glossary of terms used within the text. Words with a little number next to them will be defined in the footnote and can be found in the glossary. Plus, the glossary also includes other words that are not necessarily contained in this text but are there for reference when you need certain words defined as you continue your financial education.

As you read through the book, you will most likely discover there are some things that you will want to put into action. For this reason we've included a "To-do List" which you'll find in the back. That way, when you think,"Hmmm, I'll have to check into that," or, "I wonder if my accountant is doing that?" you have one easy place to write it down so you won't forget it!

AVOIDING TAX

One thing we have learned, working in this industry of accounting, is that people can become stuck on the expense side of the equation. While it is always advisable to be wary of expenditures and prudent with money, expenses are, and always will be, second in importance to making money.

You are far better off focusing on how to make money than focusing on reducing expenses. With this in mind, this book will teach you about investing and introduce you to business tools that can assist you in protecting your assets, while simultaneously speeding up your wealth creation by reducing your tax legally.

It is important to note at this point that here in Australia it is against the law to do something purely for the purposes of avoiding tax. If you look up "tax *evasion*" in a dictionary, you'll find it defined as illegally avoiding tax; if you then look up "tax *avoidance*", you'll see it defined as *lawful* methods of minimising tax. However, in 1981 the Australian law was changed to make tax *avoidance* illegal. You can be 100% within the law, but if you did something purely to avoid tax then it can become void. It comes under the General Anti-avoidance Rule, which is in Part 4A, "Schemes to Reduce Income Tax", of the *Income Tax Assessment Act 1936* (Cth). Therefore, whatever you do, make sure you're doing it for a valid reason, not just purely for the purposes of avoiding tax; and make sure you can substantiate that reason. In that light, you must consult a tax professional before you embark on any of the strategies outlined in this book. For more information visit www.chan-naylor.com.au

With that serious note out of the way, you're about to delve into a world where the rules are continually changing. You'll soon realise that constant learning and study is the only real weapon against anything in life. Only one thing ranks superior to knowledge and that is your attitude. Our philosophy is: never get too serious; life's a game so have fun. That may seem strange coming from us, but hey, if we can do it then so can you.

And remember, you only ever pay tax *when you make money*!

Enjoy!

Ed Chan

SPECIAL NOTICE: CHANGES IN THE LAW!

Due to the fact that the law is constantly changing, we provide updates via our free newsletter.

For more information visit

http://www.chan-naylor.com.au

PART 1:

Rules of The Game

1

The Game of Tax™

It might seem like a paradox that tax can be a game, but the truth is if you don't treat it as such you're liable to go mad. Also, games have in them a reward for overcoming challenges. The rewards only exist because the challenges are there. No challenge—no game—no fun.

Imagine what a game of football would be like if there weren't any goal posts or if there weren't any boundaries— well, you wouldn't have a game. No fun. And can youimagine trying to play a game without an opposing team? Again, no game and no fun.

And so it is with tax. The wonderful part is that there are plenty of barriers and challenges! (We can tell you're just bursting with excitement.) You see, tax is a subject which should not be taken too seriously. And you will soon discover that nobody really knows what is going on.

Tax legislation has become very complex due to constant additions and changes; for example, the Income Tax Act alone has grown from around 3000 pages in 1996 to a staggering 10,000 pages with the introduction of a "new simplified tax system". That equates to an average of more than two pages added every day for the past nine years! This added legislation has become so complex that we believe, and you can quote us, that there is probably a contradicting tax law for almost every tax law. For example, section A143-79A says "if you do it like so and so then you are okay", but a quick search will soon uncover section 2923-8791 which states "if you do it like so and so, you're in trouble". Only the immortal words of Homer Simpson can explain such a phenomenon: "Doh!"

Here's a story which highlights this fact. Apparently a test was undertaken with the participation of several reputable accountancy practices. The test was to calculate the outcome of a particular accounting scenario and submit the result. Each practice reviewed the legislation relating to the scenario and used certain methods within the legislation to calculate the outcome. A review of each submission found that they were all different. Not one had used the same method nor could they agree on the exact method to be used. Each had a valid reason for employing their methods.

Some years ago a large public mining company in Australia was hit with a demand to pay back taxes and penalties totalling $1 billion. While the mining company was acting on "the best legal advice" and stated "We don't have any tax bill", the Australian Tax Office also claimed to be acting on "the best legal advice", which said that "the mining giant does owe tax". This fight will ultimately be decided in court but it's just another example that even the "best" have no certainty on what the law actually *is* and how it is *applied*.

This realisation should let you breathe a sigh of relief as we highlight our first Tax Factor™:

- **You are not the only one who doesn't know *all* the tax laws—nobody does.**

The reason tax is so complicated is because it has evolved into a game. In the beginning, tax was something everybody tried to avoid. The government was attempting through various laws to tax everybody fairly. Some people simply broke the law and they were punished accordingly. Others got smart and found loopholes. When the loopholes were over-exploited, the laws were changed to overcome the loopholes. The game for the taxpayer became "to find a loophole" and the game for the government was to "close the loophole" with more taxation laws. There you have it; it's like a Tom and Jerry cartoon—we are playing cat and mouse. (We'll let you decide which one is the cat and which one is the mouse!)

The loopholes started with favours or exemptions for business owners or investors. As large producers and contributors to the state or country's economy, different laws provided concessions to these enterprises. Owners of such enterprises, of course, were the wealthy and although the wealthy were the original targets of tax, their cunningness allowed them to escape, relatively unaffected, leaving the rest of society to pick up the tab.

Today the game is no different. However, it seems that many have forgotten it is a game—only a few are playing. And, as with all games, the more the merrier. We invite you to play. It's legal, it's fun, it's rewarding, and it's a damn sight better than kissing goodbye to half your money! And, as you might have heard before, it's not about how much money you make over your lifetime,it's about how much you keep, and how hard that money works for you.

Those that play we call the "Players". They are the ones who understand that it's a game and learn how to use the tools of the game to their advantage. Those thatchoose not to play and continue to be affected by changes in the tax laws we call "Pawns". The only difference between the Players and the Pawns is an understanding and application of the fundamentals.

To help you grasp the fundamentals of this game, we have included a highlight of the main points—we call them "Tax Factors". The Tax Factors™ are summarised in the back of the book for quick reference and revision.

Simply knowing and using the Tax Factors will put you in the ranks of the Players, where the game becomes fun.

TAX FACTORS™

- **You are not the only one who doesn't know *all* the tax laws—nobody does.**
- **You are either a Player or a Pawn in the game of tax.**

2

The Effect of Tax

To motivate you to play the game, let's look at where you currently stand. It's no surprise that tax, by default, is simply looked upon as a bad thing. It affects every working individual in Australia. Yet its actual implications are rarely fully seen or understood. Here's an example that will help you to see the true effect tax has on your ability to advance your wealth.

COMPOUNDING[4] INTEREST

Compounding interest is the act of reinvesting your returns.[5] Let's say you have a dollar and you make a 10% return on that dollar. You have, of course, made 10 cents.

Now you have $1.10—if you make another 10% then that's 11 cents you have just made and all of a sudden your profits are getting bigger, even though you're still making a 10% return. It is like folding a piece of paper in half: the more you keep folding the paper, the thicker it gets. Each fold makes it twice as thick as before. This is the law of compounding interest and, in the finance sense, it is money making money!

---

4 **compounding**: adding to the original amount, making it larger.

5 **returns**: the income arising from assets such as property or shares.

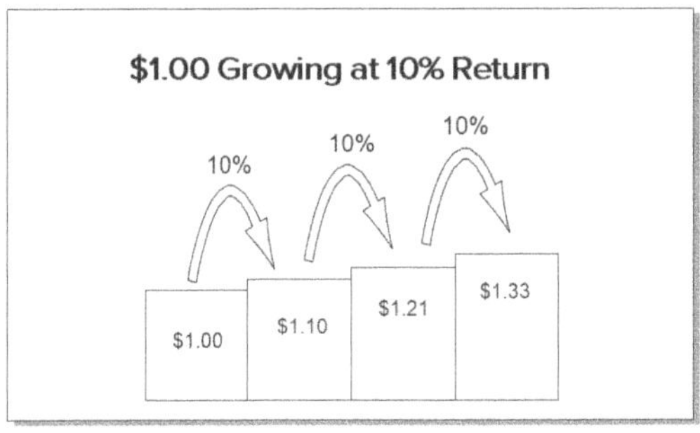

If you started with $2 and invested it at 100% return a year, this would mean that it doubles every year. In five years you would have $32, in 10 years you'd have $1024 and in 20 years, believe it or not, you'd have $1,048,576 ...!!! Over a million dollars.

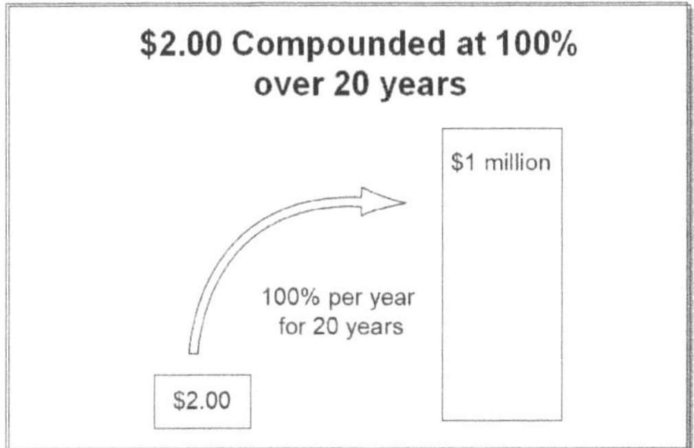

Of course, this doesn't take taxes into account. All profits are subject to tax. So what is the difference if we did take tax into account?

Given the exact same circumstances of $2 invested at 100% return a year, if you were taxed at the current highest rate of 47%, you would be left with only $5,356 after the 20-year period.

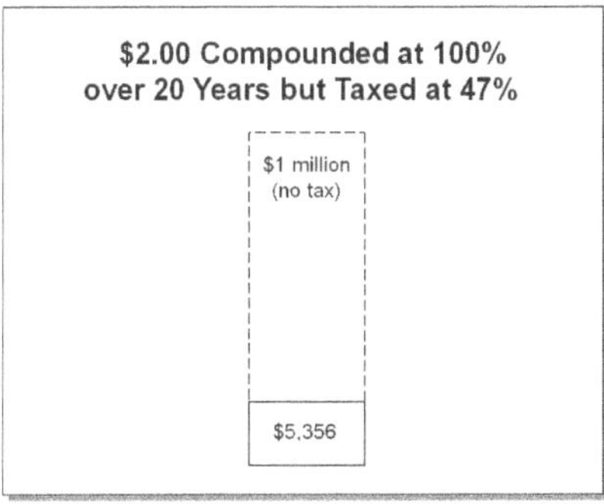

To understand the mechanics of this sobering phenomenon, take a look at the next graph. You can see how, without tax as a handicap, the $2 starts to grow rapidly after 10 years. Unhindered, the last few years really make a difference.

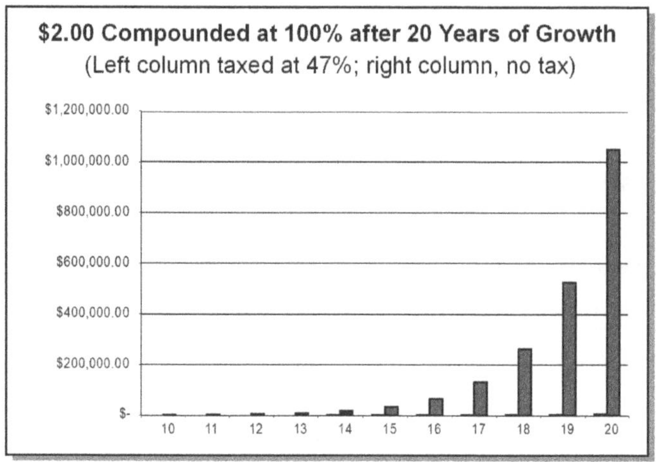

However, taxing the profits each year thwarts[6] compounding so much that the opportunity to grow exponentially[7] is lost. And so you can see how the Players get richer and the Pawns continue to struggle.

It appears to be a tough battle to "get ahead". But, as with most things in life, when you know how, it is easier.

When pointing this fact out to people, our experience is that it often results in them deciding to "never pay tax!" It's a common and understandable knee-jerk reaction and, although a solution, as far as paying tax is concerned, it's not a legal one. The sudden realisation of how much tax has and can thwart your efforts to get ahead often makes people mad at the government or the current Prime Minister. Getting mad, however, will not solve theproblem; learning the system will!

The above example of compounding $2 into a million is unrealistic because you can't pay zero tax in Australia and you don't pay 47% on every dollar—its purpose is to simply show how compounding can be dramatically affected by taking away some of the return. Depending on your circumstances, it may be possible to cap your tax rate at 30% (27.5%

6 **thwarts**: hinders or prevents (the efforts, plans or desires).
7 **exponentially**: rapidly increasing (as in size or extent) in an extreme manner.

for small business turnover under $10 million); and, for the curious readers, paying only 30% (27.5% for small business turnover under $10 million); tax in the above example would leave you with $47,814 after 20 years. While it's a tad short of a million, it's still better than $5,356!

In short, the road to wealth is faster travelled by allowing your profits to be reinvested and by learning about structures and certain tax laws. With the right knowledge and advice, you can plan your investment strategy to maximise your return while reducing your tax expenses.

3

How the Rich Play The Game

The previous chapter covered how the amount of tax you pay can, and does, hinder your ability to fast track your wealth. Reducing your tax obviously assists in compounding your returns. However, this section will show you how you can make a quantum leap and put a turbo jet engine on your wealth creation. It comes down to *when* you pay your tax.

In Australia, salary and wage earners are taxed first and then paid. It's truly amazing how as a society we've become accustomed to this. Try to explain this to a child of about five or six and they will be dumbfounded as to why people let the government take money out of their pay before they see any of it! Their innocent point of view is refreshing and thought provoking; just try it and see for yourself.

A salary earner makes his or her money, is taxed, and then spends what's left.

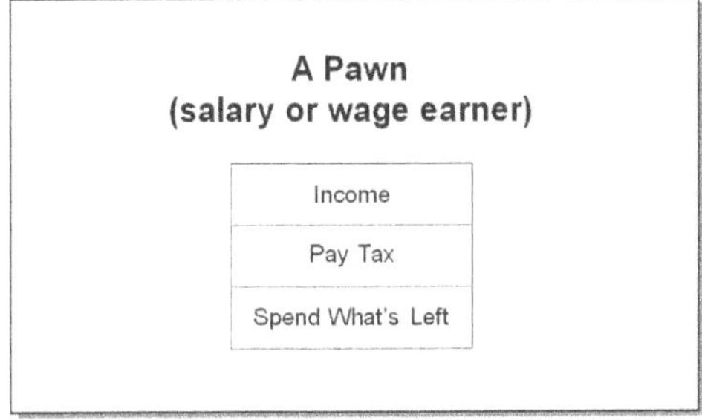

A Player will do it differently. They will make money, spend it on legitimate expenses and then pay tax on what is left.

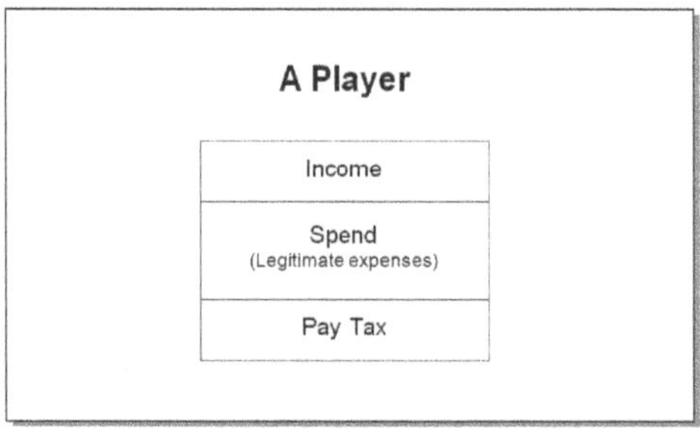

The table below shows the difference between asalary earner and someone who uses the system when they both earn $100,000.

Pawn (salaryearner)		Player	
Income	$100,000	Income	$100,000
		Spend (legitimate expenses)	$40,000
		Taxable Income	$60,000
Tax Paid (Approx)	$32,000	Tax Paid (Approx)	$14,800
Net Income	$68,000	Net Income	$45,200
Spending Capacity	$68,000	Spending Capacity	$85,200

Just by being able to claim certain expenses and pay them before they are taxed has created an extra $17,200 for the Player.

This is often considered too simple and thus overlooked, but the sooner you get into the position of a Player, the more leverage you will have with which to play the game.

Despite its simplicity, remember this Tax Factor:

- **A Player gets paid first.**

4

The Self-assessment System

It may come as quite a revelation to you when you realise that the responsibility for a true and correct tax return rests on your shoulders, even if your accountant did your tax return for you.

In Australia, we have a self-assessment tax system. The responsibility of claiming deductions and submitting a tax return is up to the individual. Even if you have an accountant, you are still fully responsible for a 100% correct and accurately lodged tax return. This might surprise you, but if you look closely at any tax form prepared by an accountant, you'll see a declaration that looks like this:

> "I, [your name], declare that the information in this tax return is true and correct."

And the accountant's declaration usually goes something like this:

> "I, of [firm name], declare that this return has been prepared in accordance with the information supplied by the taxpayer, that the taxpayer has given me a declaration stating the information provided to me is true and correct and that the taxpayer has authorised me to lodge the tax return."

Despite the accountant being the one who has gone to college or university for several years, who then also served an apprenticeship under a licensed tax agent, you are the one who is held responsible for a correct tax return—regardless of your education. The accountant is the one with the *qualification* but the onus[8] rests with you!

This, we believe, is the reason for a complicated and suppressive tax system. The reason we describe it as "suppressive" is because under this system the might of the government is bearing down upon the individual. This, in itself, is overwhelming and creates a "there's nothing I can do about it" state of mind in an individual. In addition to this, although full responsibility lies with the individual, no means of public education exists to teach a person how the system works. Ignorance is the best way to control a person; it creates a trap in itself. Give a child the keys to your car and let them drive it without practice or education and they'll wind up in a mess. The child would probably get so overwhelmed after a near miss or collision that they'd refuse to drive a car again for a long time, if at all. So not teaching somebody about something breeds ignorance, confusion and a lack of understanding, which ultimately leads to no action in that area or zone. And so it is with tax. It is a complex, difficult system which is not explained to those who are affected by it throughout their lives and who are then made responsible for it if it's wrong. That is why the word "suppressive" is used.

The end result is an individual who works hard and receives, in many cases, only two-thirds of their money for their efforts, and the more they produce, the more they are paralysed. Without an understanding of the system and how to use it legally, the disheartened worker will choose one of the following techniques in an effort to pay less tax:

1. Take advantage of tax schemes and lose money.
2. Not do extra work or not work at all.
3. Illegally transact with cash dealings and not declare income.

Thus, you have a gradient scale downwards where, in today's society, the top is legal and the bottom is criminal.

---

8 **onus**: a duty or responsibility; burden.

If a society is continually suppressed by the tax system and remains ignorant of how to prosper within the law, then we are heading for a society that sees no benefit in trying harder to raise standards or go that extra mile. And when this same society takes from those who produce and gives it to those who don't—that's the last straw that breaks the Pawn's back. Why bother even working at all? An individual who works hard feels better about themselves than one who has lazed about all day. Sure, we all like to take a break now and then but to constantly reward somebody for doing nothing produces a freeloader. The result is that such people become more parasitic, expecting more the less they do. A society that advocates helping those who do nothing by taking from those who work hard and produce, is a society that is on a downward spiral of inefficiency and ineffectiveness.

At the risk of appearing philosophical or, heaven forbid, even political, what we're saying is a fact. Take a walk through the dole-ridden streets scattered around Australia; you'll see for yourself—desperation, drugs, violence and criminality. Giving somebody something for nothing is about one of the cruellest things you can do to that person, and they'll hate you for it.

If we want to create a wealthy country and if we want to build a society that produces abundance, then we must start educating ourselves and our youth.

Of course, money is not everything, but say that to a poor, hungry or desperate person and they're liable to disagree. Having money gives you choices and the ability to help. But when money is scarce it reduces your choices and affects your own survival.

The thing that you have the least of, and want, is the most important thing to *you*. It might be money one day or a kiss from your sweetheart the next. Our needs and wants change but, as a wise man once said, "Poor people don't build hospital wings."

If you want to help your family, friends and fellow man, you need to be able to work and produce.

Understanding business, marketing, investing and finance is necessary in order to make money. Understanding the tax laws helps you to keep it. And the first step is realising it *is* your responsibility—it's up to you!

▸Legal tax reduction ... It's up to you!

The basic concept of tax is not complicated; take a little from each person to fund roads, schools, transport and improve society's survival in general through healthcare and research. It's fairly simple when you look at it that way. But it has been made complicated and this is why it becomes suppressive—because the individual taxpayer cannot understand it. For instance, take this example, a section of the tax code:

> "For the purpose of calculating the attributable safe harbour excess amount in section 820-920(4) of the Income Tax Assessment Act 1997 ('ITAA 1997'), can a Step 1 amount, which is zero, when reduced by a negative adjusted average debt amount give rise to a positive Step 2 amount?"

Insane!

When you take a bird's eye view of the whole tax system, and manage to straighten out the mass of confusion and make something of it, the immediate realisation is that it seems very unfair. And that *is* how it is—unfair and unjust.

Now, that has a tendency to make people feel a little mad. However, you can prosper and stay within the law and you don't need to be super rich or even rich—all you need is to understand it and apply what you know.

Like most things, it's easy when you know. And here's some information that will get you on the right track ...

▸ You never invest or willingly lose money just to get a tax deduction. Never.

Violation of this principle is why so many people wound up in trouble with all those tax schemes, involving such things as tree plantations and ostrich farms that, for the sake of an immediate loss, promised long-term growth. Not all of these schemes have been made illegal but where they have been made illegal, the people involved are now being made to pay back the tax which they avoided. This is not the way the game is played.

We know of people who purposely keep their properties negatively geared just to get a tax deduction. This shows a total misunderstanding of how to play the game. Negative gearing has its place; often the rental market and your initial downpayment just aren't enough to cover all expenses, so in the first year or two or maybe more, you have to put some cash in yourself. But you would never purposely continue this if it was possible to actually generate an income.

It's amusing to see a person's reaction when they complain about paying more tax and you point out to them "You're only paying more tax because you're earning more money!" You see them suddenly realise "Oh yeah, I forgot about that."

People get stuck on one side of the equation—tax, tax, tax. That is probably why our tax events are so popular.

The truth is, there are only two ways to play the game of tax. You don't play the game by dealing only in cash, and you certainly don't do it by making less money. The way to play is:

- **You make tons of money and either:**
  1. **Have a business; or**
  2. **Invest.**

These are MUSTS—business owner or investor (or both). Only then does the game become playable, only then does it become fun.

If you remain an employee (and don't invest), you remain a Pawn in the game. You're the one who feels the pinch of the government's budgets and "New Tax Systems". The Players don't feel them.

Why is it so? Because the tax laws have evolved that way. A long time ago, when tax was introduced, those that provided wealth for the village, the country and forsociety in general were given a helping hand. The wealthy were given tax concessions when their contributions benefited the society and government of that time.

After all, a business owner provides jobs; an investor provides opportunity, or housing for people to live in. Their contribution is rewarded with different tax laws.

Of course, that's not to say that an employee doesn't contribute, quite the contrary. Nurses, doctors, teachers,tradespeople—all these and everyone else working insociety has a vital role. But the tax laws don't recognisethem; they only recognise the business owner andinvestor.

Playing the game requires a lot more than keeping a few receipts so that you can add up your tax deductions. Business owners and investors learn about and use structures such as companies and trusts. These legal entities have additional benefits such as asset protection, lower tax rates and income distribution. These entities have different tax laws.

In order to use the tax laws legally, one must learn how the system works. To begin, you need to know and understand the two main taxes ...

TAX FACTORS

- **Legal tax reduction ... It's up to you!**
- **You never invest or willingly lose money just to get a tax deduction. Never.**
- **To play the game of tax you need to be either a business owner or an investor (or both).**

5

The Two Main Taxes

Before we delve into the tools of the game—namely, companies and trust structures—it is necessary to show you how to keep score. You need to know if you are winning at this game called tax. You do this by measuring the differences in tax rates between an individual and a company or trust.

Income tax is money taken out of your salary before you see it. The more you earn, the higher the rate. The table below shows the Australian personal income tax rates.

Income Tax Rates Table

Income Bracket (2017/2018)	Tax Rate
$0 – $18,200	Nil
$18,201– $37,000	19%*
$37,001 – $87,000	32.5%*
$87,001 – $180,000	37%*
$180,001 +	45%*

*Plus Medicare levy which is normally calculated at 2% of your taxable incomebut this rate may vary depending on your circumstances. Throughout this book 47% is quoted as the highest tax bracket, which is the highest income tax rateof 45% plus the Medicare levy. *Please note that these rates can change from year to year. Visit www.ato.gov.au for more information.*

THE TWO DIFFERENT TYPES OF RETURN

As mentioned, in order to play the game of tax, you have to be an investor or own a business. There is no other way.

And whether business owner or investor, it's worth knowing what ROI means. For most, it means Return On Investment. But that's only half of it.

The term ROI is an acronym for two phrases:
Return *Of* Investment = A measurement of time
Return On Investment = A dollar amount or percentage

An investor needs to know and understand both.

RETURN OF INVESTMENT

Return *Of* Investment will determine if the investment is worth doing at all. It's the answer to the question: "How long before I get my money back?"

When comparing investment options, one considers opportunity cost, by calculating whether a better return can be made elsewhere. Having money tied up too long can mean money is lost on other opportunities. Knowing *when* you will get your money back can help assess the viability of the investment.

Return Of Investment affects the savvy[9] investor when considering the tax implications.

RETURN ON INVESTMENT

Return *On* Investment is the amount you receive for risking your cash. Savvy investors always get paid when taking a risk.

The amount of money you save on tax can be considered a Return *On* Investment. The cost of establishing the correct structure, getting the right advice and self-education are all, to some extent, an investment where the return can be quantified in the amount of tax saved over the long term.

The formula for ROI is:
Sale Price – Dollar Investment = ROI as a dollar amount (ROI $ / Investment $) x 100 = ROI as a percentage

9 **savvy**: having a sophisticated understanding; well informed.

MONEY COSTS MONEY

No matter what you do with your money, it costs you money. Let's explain.

If you borrow money from a bank, they may charge 7% interest—that means that the money costs you 7%. Let's look at your income that way. Let's say you pay 47% in tax, which means income costs you 47%. When you earn another dollar then you pay 47% for that dollar. If you borrowed, however, you'd only pay 7%. That's why some of the world's billionaires don't earn an income; they live off their equity because it's cheaper money! It's an application of the ROI principle.

TWO TYPES OF RETURNS

When considering the return on investment as an amount, there are two types of returns an investor considers:

1. Capital Growth.
2. Income.

In Australia, income and capital growth (or gain) are taxed differently. It depends largely on how long an investment is held. Thus, we have two different categories of investor.

INVESTOR CATEGORIES

To help clarify what type of tax is paid on profits from investing, a general rule of thumb can be applied:

Trader—is one who buys and sells within a 12-month period.
Long-term investor—is one who holds on to an asset for more than 12 months.

A trader pays income tax; the long-term investor pays capital gains tax. This is a simple way of differentiating between the two.

CAPITAL GAIN

Capital is the amount of money contributed to the purchase of an asset, such as a house, business or shares. When the asset appreciates, the investment has gained more capital. If the asset is sold, the capital gain, which is the value the asset increased by, is subject to tax. This is called capital gains tax, or CGT.

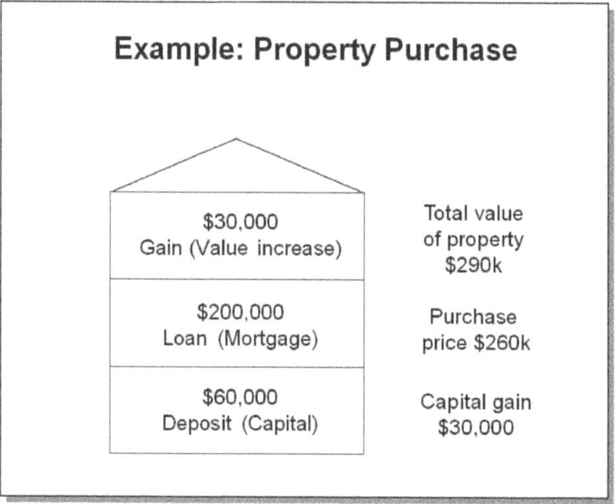

Under current tax law, the capital gain above ($30,000) is subject to capital gains tax (CGT) unless it is your own home. The rate of CGT is the same as your income tax rate. But if you owned the investment for more than 12 months, you get a 50% discount on the capital gain. So if your gain was $50,000 you only pay tax on $25,000 of that gain, as long as you owned the investment for over a year.

Assuming the income tax rate was 30% and the investment was owned for two years, in the above example the CGT would be $30,000 less the 50% discount =$15,000x30%=$4500.

At this point, it is worth mentioning that the amount of tax you end up paying is dependent upon forward planning.

Structuring yourself correctly in the beginning can save you thousands. It is usually too late to do something when you already own an investment or have made a profit. One gentleman comes to mind who was seeking counsel about this very thing. He was in the "unfortunate" predicament of having made over a million dollars on some shares he had purchased. Because he purchased them in his own name, he was reluctant to sell, knowing he would lose nearly $250,000 in CGT. This delay cost him more because the share price reversed, halving his gain. Had he been correctly structured, the CGT would have been dramatically reduced.

Usually, when people realise the difference between CGT and income tax and that CGT is relative to income tax, they immediately conclude that if they earned no income then the CGT would be zero. Although this is a logical and sensible consideration, it is unfortunately not the case. If, during a financial year, you receive no income but a large capital gain, the capital gain would be taxed as income, after the 50% discount, providing you owned the asset for more than 12 months.

Please note that CGT does not apply to investment properties purchased prior to September 1985.

TAX FACTORS

- **The term ROI is an acronym for two phrases:**
- **Return *Of* Investment is measured in the *time* it takes to return your investment.**
- **Return *On* Investment is measured in a dollar amount or percentage.**

PART 2:

A Player's Tools

6

Tools of The Game

There is another important concept that must be understood before we delve into the different types of structures. This will make all the difference if you grasp it. An investor or business owner has tools. These are such things as structures and the ROI concept. These *are* tools. Although not as apparent as a drill or a screwdriver, they are nevertheless just as vital in the game of tax.

What would your reaction be to a tradesman trying to cut a piece of wood in half without a saw or an axe? Imagine if this tradesman went around the neighbourhood asking people how to cut this piece of wood. Let's say that out of frustration the tradesman takes a standard household kitchen knife, the kind you use to eat your dinner with, and starts sawing! Well, he's not going to get very far, is he?

What would happen when you showed him a saw or, better still, a power saw? Boy, would he be relieved if he'd just started out. However, he might be very frustrated if he'd already toiled and strained and actually cut through the wood with a blunt knife, only to discover the job could have been done in one-tenth of the time with much less effort.

And so it is with the tools of investing!

The result you're aiming for might be asset protection or less tax or both. Speed and effectiveness are determined by your understanding and usage of structures, in combination with an evaluation of your ROI. These are the tools you employ to maximise your efforts and money, just like a power saw cutting through wood.

INVESTING SEQUENCE™

These tools, however, are conceptual; they are not as evident as a hammer or drill and consequently get overlooked, only to be put into use after the deal has been done, which is often too late.

Therefore, a Player must realise that the *sequence* the tools are used in, affects the overall outcome. Using our tradesman example; it is much harder to drive a screw into a piece of hardwood with no hole already made. You can sweat and toil for hours on such a task. If one were to first drill a hole into the wood, driving in a screw would then be much easier. The effort and time of putting in the screw is reduced by using the right tool first.

The Player who invests or goes into business should utilise his or her tools in a sequence that strengthens and protects the assets. The following diagram shows the most appropriate sequence for investing or starting a business.

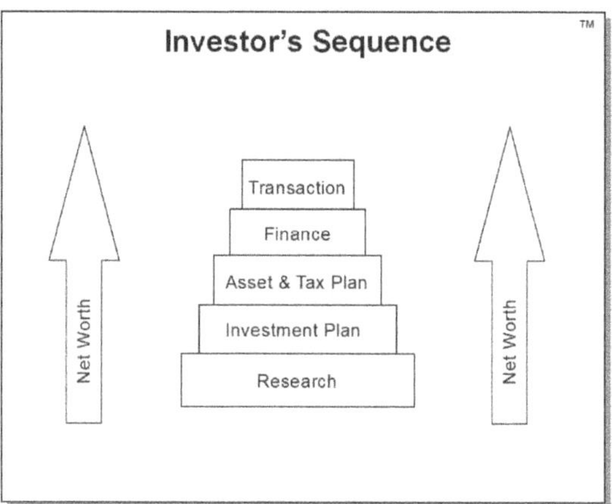

Each building block of wealth is self-explanatory. Before investing, the Player does their research, whether it's for a business or an investment. Then they plan whether the investment is long term or short term, keeping in mind the ROI. When that's all figured out, the Player then visits their accountant and works out the asset protection and tax plan. Only then does the Player organise finance and follow through with the investment transaction (buy or sell), or start business production.

It would be ludicrous to change the sequence and buy the asset, get the finance and do the research. This is obvious. Yet people will go ahead and skip the first three steps, which is just as crazy. In fact, missing out a building block is just as bad as doing it out of sequence.

And what we find all too often is this:

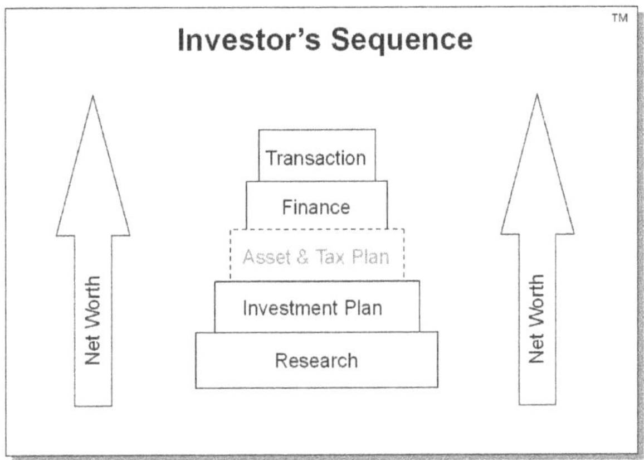

No asset protection or tax planning has been considered and the pyramid is consequently weakened through this lack of asset and tax planning.

Instead, the accountant is consulted afterwards, usually at tax time. This is not a plea to visit accountants more regularly out of a desire to be considered more popular. (We've heard all the accountant jokes, you know!) It is much more serious than that because the result can be costly. Skipping a building block is not recommended. It is just like building a house in real life: if you skimp on the foundations, the rest can come tumbling down—which, in this analogy, you'll see reduces your net worth. An earthquake can bring down a building if its foundations are weak; likewise, getting sued or being involved in a bad financial investment or business deal could be the equivalent of an earthquake. If your building blocks are solid then you may see it through relatively unharmed, but if any one of those blocks is weak, it can bring the whole lot down. The point is, that it can cost you money doing it out of sequence.

It is interesting to note that those we know who have done this out of sequence (and they are many) and missed the asset planning and tax step, inevitably end up having to redo the steps from tax planning on up, including refinancing and a re-transaction. (Transferring an asset into a trust, for example, is the same as selling the asset to the trust and is considered a transaction.)

The next most common scenario we see is this:

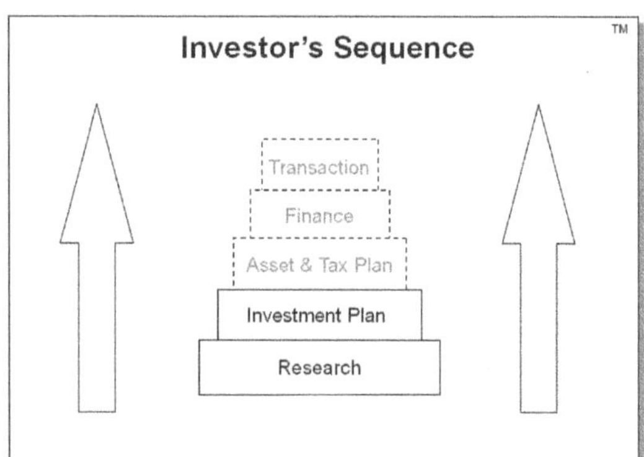

Lots of research and planning but no further actions. It can be a little frightening buying your first investment or going into business yourself; however, one mustovercome any fear and push right on through. The rewards are there for those who persistently pursue their dreams. You are the only one who really stands in your way. Just like a building is only ever built by *action,* block by block, with the end goal in mind, so too is the realisation of your financial dreams.

The Investor Sequence applies to *every* investing transaction (or business establishment) not just the firstone. And it applies to selling and not just buying.

So remember—understanding and using the tools of the game in the right sequence makes it easier to play. And just so you know where you are in the game, the following diagram shows the Scale of Tax Tools™. It reiterates the point that only as a business owner or investor can you really play the game. The purpose of this scale is to show you the effectiveness of the different tools available and also what methods you should avoid. Use it as a guide for where you are and as a plan for what to learn next.

TAX FACTORS

- **The tools of the tax game consist of structures, the ROI concept and future planning.**
- **The Player always follows the Investor's Sequence™.**

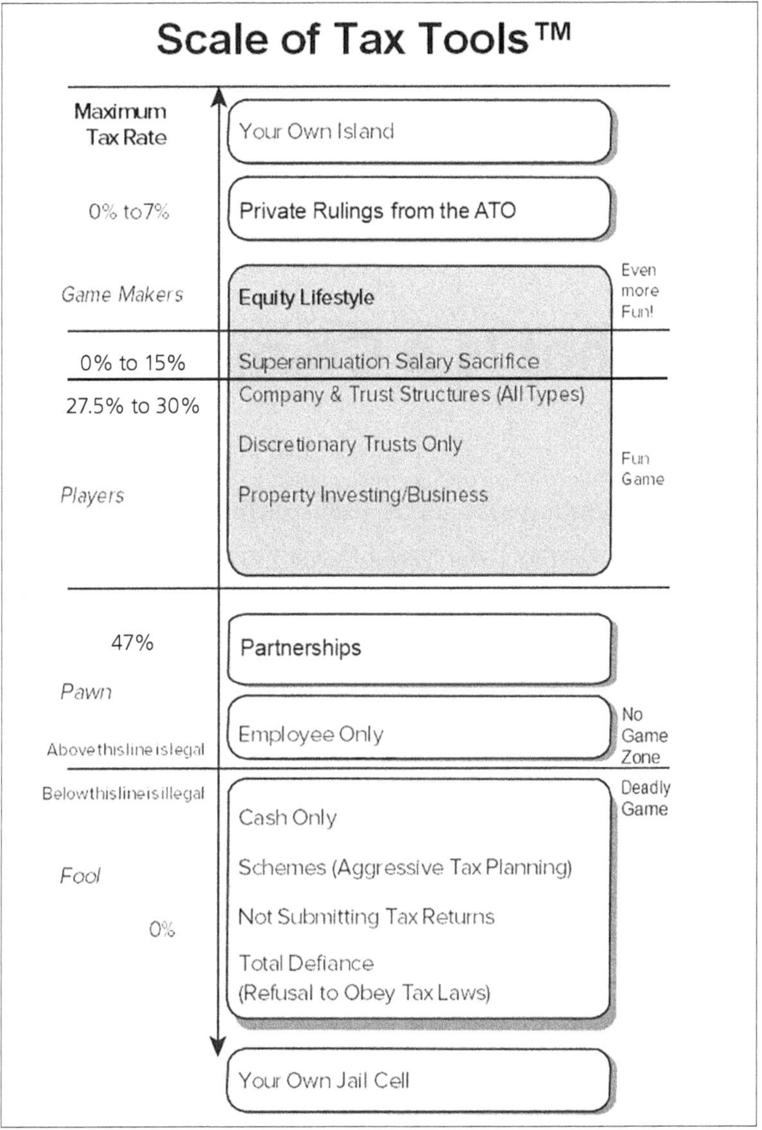
Scale of Tax Tools™
Maximum Tax Rate
Your Own Island
0% to7%
Private Rulings from the ATO
Game Makers
Equity Lifestyle
Even more Fun!
0% to 15%
Superannuation Salary Sacrifice
27.5% to 30%
Company & Trust Structures (All Types)
Discretionary Trusts Only
Players
Property Investing/Business
Fun Game
47%
Partnerships
Pawn
Employee Only
No Game Zone
Above this line is legal
Below this line is illegal
Deadly Game
Cash Only
Fool
Schemes (Aggressive Tax Planning)
0%
Not Submitting Tax Returns
Total Defiance
(Refusal to Obey Tax Laws)
Your Own Jail Cell

7

What Is a Company?

The first thing to know about a company structure is that it is a completely separate legal entity. It is treated differently to an individual. A company is subject to different tax laws. As far as the TaxDepartment is concerned, it is another person—without a soul.

ANATOMY OF A COMPANY

A company consists of several roles and is broken up into shares.

Directors: Control the company's day-to-day running and are responsible for keeping the company solvent. This includes future planning for continual expansion. A company can have one or many directors. Large corporations[10] often have a board of directors who decide by a majority vote. In short, directors are those who direct the company.

Secretary: Responsible for the administration of the company. A secretary is officially appointed to ensure correspondence and records are maintained. The role is extremely important in medium and large organisations but in the case of an individual operation, it is more of a legal tradition than anything else. After all, in a company established by a single individual, that person ends up being the director, the secretary, and the only shareholder.

---

10 **corporation:** another name for a company.

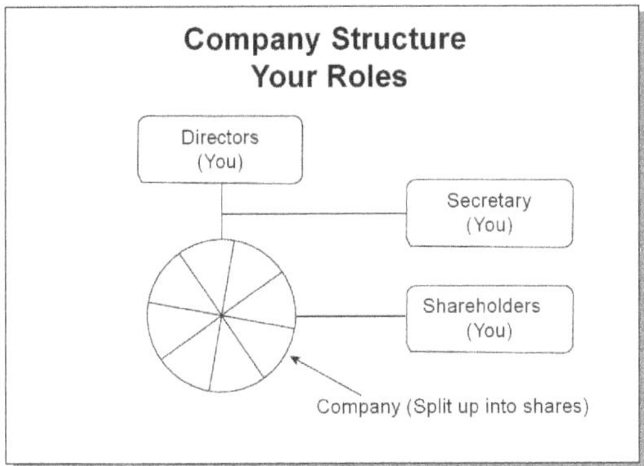

Shareholders: A company is split into portions; much like a pizza is cut into slices. A company can be split into two shares or into millions of shares. Owners of these shares are called shareholders.

The person with the most shares generally controls the company. A shareholder can be a director but doesn't have to be. A majority shareholder can appoint a director to run the company. At the directors' discretion, shareholders can receive a share in the profits of the company; this is known as a dividend.

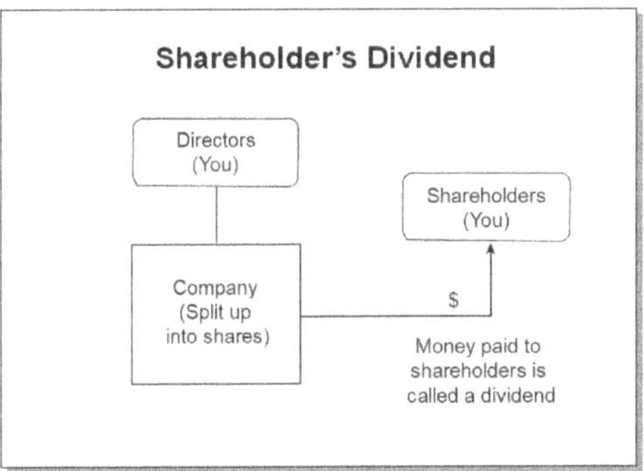

Directors are legally responsible for what happens with the company. Should the company fall into bankruptcy, the directors can be held responsible. In our environment of ever increasing litigation, where a select few are trying to earn a quick buck by suing someone wealthy, a proprietary limited[11] company

11 **Proprietary limited**: proprietary is relating to an owner or ownership. Proprietary limited is a type of company whose ownership is limited to a certain amount of shares and shareholders; commonly abbreviated to "Pty Ltd". A company that has no restrictions on ownership is normally listed on the stock exchange where its shares can be purchased by anyone; this is called a Limited type company and will have the abbreviation "Ltd" after its name.

doesn't protect the directors if the company is sued. Therefore, directors of companies are wise to use asset protection precautions, especially if they are in an industry that commonly suffers unjust litigation claims of negligence.

COMPANY TAX RATE

One of the main differences between an individual and a company is the tax rate. A company pays 30% (or 27.5% for trading company turnover under $10m) tax whether it earns one dollar or a million dollars. Therefore, a company has an immediate advantage over an individual who is in the 47% tax bracket (see the table in Chapter 5 — "The Two Main Taxes").

Through sensible planning, income tax can be limited to 30% (or 27.5% for trading company turnover under $10m). This, of course, doesn't apply to an employee, but for an investor or business owner it may be possible.

DISADVANTAGES OF USING A COMPANY STRUCTURE

There are, however, some disadvantages to a company structure. First, the 50% CGT discount is not available to a company, only to an individual. (Even so, CGT paid canbe used to the advantage of directors or shareholders at a laterdate.)

Furthermore, income can only be taken out as:

a. Wages
b. Director's fees
c. Director's bonuses or
d. Dividends.

Whenever a company pays wages, director's fees or bonuses, in addition to being subject to income tax, the income is also subject to workers compensation and superannuation payments. Depending on the industry type, this could mean a 10% to 24% additional cost on wages, director's fees or bonuses.

Dividends are not subject to workers compensation or superannuation but they are NOT tax deductible[12] to the company. Income tax must be paid by the shareholder receiving dividends, at the shareholder's tax rate.

12 **tax deductible**: able to be claimed against income.

Sometimes the company will pay 30% (or 27.5% for trading company turnover under $10m) tax on the dividend before it pays it to the shareholder. In this case, the shareholder is considered to have paid 30% (or 27.5% for trading company turnover under $10m) tax already on the dividends received. If the shareholder's tax rate is 47% then he or she will need to pay an additional 17% (or 19.5%) to make up the difference. If, however, the shareholder's tax rate is only 15% then they will be refunded the extra 15% tax paid.

You can, of course, leave the money in the company and pay 30% (or 27.5% for trading company turnover under $10m) tax; only when you take it out do these above rules apply.

Also, from a shareholder's perspective, a company doesn't necessarily offer complete asset protection, which we'll explain more about later. Lastly, there are, of course, the legal and accounting costs involved in establishing and maintaining a company.

All of these points must be considered if one is going to use a company as an investment or business vehicle. One would consider using a company when the advantages outweigh the disadvantages per the numbers. It's generally a calculation of the amount of tax saved at 30% (or 27.5% for trading company turnover under $10m) compared to 47%, minus the extra costs associated with establishing and running a company. This is basically an application of working out your ROI.

As always, you need to see a tax professional before embarking upon the use of a company structure as each person's circumstances are different.

8

What Is a Trust?

A trust is basically an agreement or promise. A person or company agrees to hold assets for the benefit of another. The one who holds the assets is called the trustee; those who benefit are called beneficiaries. The trustee has legal control;[13] it's the trustee's name that appears on all legal documents, bank accounts, etc. The beneficiaries are not mentioned on such documents and have beneficial ownership,[14] meaning that they are entitled to the assets and profits of the trust. The basic function of a trust is to separate control and ownership.

There are many different types of trusts. The important thing to note is that different trusts are used for different purposes. There is no "one-size-fits-all" when it comes to structures. As already mentioned, it depends on your individual situation.

Although there are many more types, the following are the more commonly used trusts.

---

13 **legal control:** legal title only. A person with legal control can buy and sell an asset but will never own or enjoy the benefits of ownership (such as income or usage).

14 **beneficial ownership**: Allowing a person to enjoy the benefits of ownership (including usage, income, profits etc) even though legal title is in another name.

DISCRETIONARY TRUST

Discretionary describes the ability to choose or judge. A Discretionary Trust allows the trustee to decide who gets what! The trustee has full discretion to distribute both income and capital to whoever it decides and can vary it from year to year.

UNIT TRUST

A Unit Trust is split up into units, much like a company is split up into shares. Profits and income are distributed via the units to the individual. Unit Trusts are very useful, especially for property investors and investors with Self- Managed Super Funds.

HYBRID TRUST

The word "hybrid" means "made from a mixed origin"; biologically, it refers to crossbreeding. Hence, a Hybrid Trust is a cross between a Discretionary and a Unit Trust. This type of structure is quite appealing because it includes the benefits of both and so is an extremely useful structure for business and investing.

ANATOMY OF A DISCRETIONARY TRUST

This chapter explains Discretionary Trusts. This is often the type of trust talked about when someone says "I have a trust". Unit and Hybrid Trusts are discussed in a later chapter.

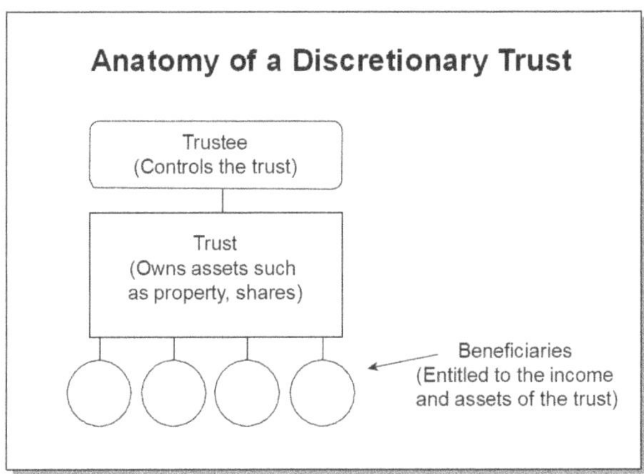

A trust consists of trustees, beneficiaries and assets.

TRUSTEE

A trustee can be a single person or a group of people or acompany. The trustee does not own anything; their role isprimarily one of decision making. The trustee makes all the decisions regarding the buying and selling of assets,the allocation of profits (to beneficiaries) and the spending of money in general.

The assets and profits of a trust belong to neither the trustee nor the beneficiaries; they are *owned by the trust.* The assets are held "in trust" that they'll be looked after for the future benefit of the beneficiaries, hence the word trustee.

Historically, trusts were used by the wealthy who, knowing they were close to the grave, would establish a trust for their children. Money and assets were left under the control of an appointed trustee until such time as the children reached an age where they could take responsibility for the wealth themselves. As time progressed, trusts were then utilised for legal protection for those in highly risky endeavours, such as ocean sailing and exploration. The utilisation of such entities provided the trustee with limited liability should a ship and her crew be lost at sea. The assets, such as the ships and cargo, were protected by trusts. This allowed the trustees to avoid large payouts to the families of those who died or went missing at sea. Thus, asset protection was born.

The more common scenario today is that the trustee is also a beneficiary; however, the trustee can only be a beneficiary if there are other beneficiaries.

BENEFICIARIES

The beneficiaries are entitled to the assets and profits of the trust. The allocation of these is up to the trustee; it is at the trustee's discretion that funds are distributed.

Just because someone is a beneficiary doesn't mean that they will definitely receive profits from the trust. In fact, a beneficiary may not receive anything at all. Only when the trustee decides to pass profits on to a beneficiary, does that person or entity receive anything. A beneficiary can be a person, company, charity, religious organisation or even another trust.

INCOME SPLITTING

Income or profits can be allocated to any of the beneficiaries. For example, $1200 could be split equally among three beneficiaries so that each receives $400, or one beneficiary could receive $600 and the others receive $300 each. It is entirely up to the trustee who gets what.

The important point to note is that tax is paid by the beneficiary and is based on the beneficiary's total income, including any income from the trust. This is where there is an immediate benefit, because the trustee has a choiceand can choose to distribute the income to the lower income earner; thereby, less tax is paid on the money than if it was given to the higher income earner.

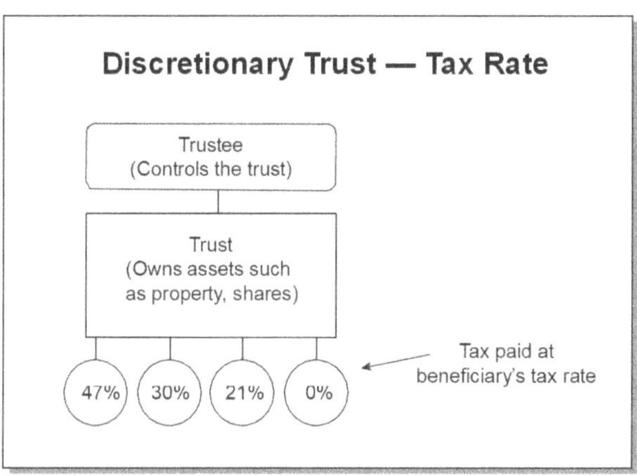

BENEFICIARIES UNDER 18 YEARS

Usually people immediately conclude that having four children enables them to utilise the tax-free threshold of $18,200 for each child[15], plus low income tax offset allowing them to earn $20,500 tax free. However, in an effort to reduce the exploitation of giving money to beneficiaries under 18 years old, the government introduced a new law.

Income received by those under the age of 18, which is not directly related to personal exertion (actually working to earn the money), is subject to a penalty tax rate. The first $416 received by a minor is tax free, but any additional income is subject to a tax rate of 66% (ouch!) up to $1307. Any extra income above $1307 is taxed at 45%.

15 **tax-free threshold**: referring to the amount of tax-free money that can be earned in a single year. See Income Tax Rates Table in Chapter 5.

So gone are the days of rich Uncle Joe giving newlybornJohnny$18,200 (or $20,500 with low income tax offset) tax-free income. Unfortunately, Uncle Joe has to wait until Johnny is 18 years old before he can utilise him as a beneficiary.

CHARITY AND RELIGIONS

Usually, depending on how the trust is set up, the trustee is able to distribute funds to charities and religious organisations, thereby supporting their favourite charity or local church with donations. Most charities and religions are exempt from income tax and therefore any funds given to such institutions from a trust can be considered tax free.

ASSETS

The assets of a trust can be anything: property, shares, businesses, art—you name it. The main point to realise is that the trust owns the assets, not you and not the trustee.

FINANCING THROUGH A TRUST

A trust can borrow money just like a company or a person. Some people find that borrowing through a trust reduces the number of potential lenders and their willingness to lend. From our experience, this is simply from ignorance as to what a trust is. If you approach three different people from the same bank, you are likely to get three different opinions in respect to lending to a trust. Generally, your typical front counter person doesn't know how to organise a loan for a trust. You need to approach a senior and more experienced lending manager in the bank, who understands what a trust is and has experience in lending to trusts. Using the assets of the trust as security is simply a third party mortgage.[16]

If the trust cannot substantiate income requirements to finance a loan then a personal guarantee[17] is most likely necessary. This, of course, is no

16 **third party mortgage**: when a loan is guaranteed by someone else's assets, other than the assets of the person taking out the loan.

17 **personal guarantee:** the permission for a financial institution to claim your personal assets and income should the entity which borrowed the money (such as a trust or company) become unable to pay the loan.

different than if you were financing it yourself anyway. Once a trust is making regular income and can prove it, borrowing without a personal guarantee becomes possible.

TAX RATE

Fundamentally, a trust doesn't have a tax rate per se. There is, however, a penalty tax for not distributing all the profits. Any profits left in the trust are subject to 45% tax. So, in essence, you are forced to distribute profits to the beneficiaries.

ESTABLISHING A TRUST

When you establish a trust, you receive a copy of the trust deed,[18] which is a legal document that explains in detail what you can and cannot do with the trust. The word "deed" originates from an Old English word which means "do or act". Information, such as who is the trustee and who are the beneficiaries, is included in the deed. The deed must be signed by all parties involved. For it to be valid, it must also be officially stamped by the local Office of State Revenue;[19] this is normally organised by the accountant or solicitor who establishes the trust on your behalf.

One unusual role is that of the settlor; this is someone who puts down a sum of money to start the trust, commonly around $10. Once the trust is established, the settlor has no other role, entitlements, rights or connection to the trust. This is akin to the old days when Grandpa Joe would set up a trust for the young ones, put in some money and get his friend to look after it until the young ones were older.

APPOINTOR

The appointor (sometimes called the principal) has, in fact, the most powerful role in a trust and should be carefully selected. While the trustee is the one who decides what happens to the assets, funds and profits of the trust, it is the appointor who has the power to change the trustee and appoint

---

18 **deed:** a signed document that outlines the terms of an agreement.

19 **Office of State Revenue:** a department of state government that administers the state taxation, and collects revenue, outstanding fines and penalties. See glossary for a list of the websites for each office.

a new one. They are like gods in the area of trusts. Therefore, make sure when establishing a trust that you have two appointors—yourself and someone else who you can trust. The reason for this is that the changing of appointors can be costly and by having two appointors,
the death of one doesn't create any additional costs.

COMPANY AS TRUSTEE

One of the downsides to a Discretionary Trust is that if the individual who is the trustee suddenly dies, then the trust's assets can be subject to stamp duty[20] if they get transferred to the beneficiaries. The reason for this is that the legal name recorded on a property, for example, will have to be changed. One method of overcoming this is by having a company as the trustee. The directors of the company run the trust. This way, the company will always remain trustee, only the directors will change.

Under such a set-up, you then have several roles; in addition to being a beneficiary and the appointor of the trust, you are also the director and shareholder of the trustee company.

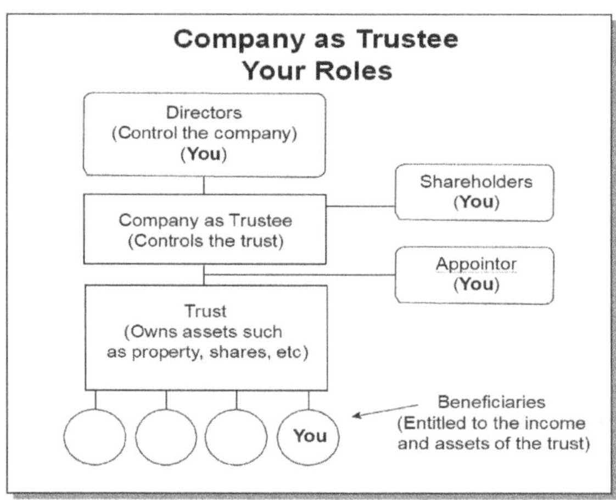

Structures like this one above are how Players protect and pass on their wealth, from generation to generation, without tax implications. You see, the trustee company doesn't own anything and therefore the shares are

20 **stamp duty**: a duty (or tax) applied to some legal documents, especially on transfer of ownership. A stamp is fixed to a document to show that the duty has been paid and the transfer is valid.

worthless. When it comes to transferring assets, the only thing that gets transferred is the shares, which might be worth $2. There could be a billion dollars in that trust but a transfer of the $2 shares gives the new owner control over the whole lot. The way it works is, the new shareholder makes himself (or herself) a director and then has full control with no stamp duty incurred[21] on the trust's assets.

QUARANTINED[22] LOSSES

A special tax ruling allows losses on investment property to be offset against personal income. However, we often find that people, in an effort to protect their assets, have established a Discretionary Trust to purchase investment property. This is not recommended, especially if the property is negatively geared, because the negative gearing losses get trapped inside the Discretionary Trust. Losses cannot be passed on to beneficiaries to be deducted against personal income and so must remain inside the trust until it eventually makes an income to offset against any losses.

Also, in New South Wales, the Discretionary Trust is unfairly treated in regards to land tax and receives no land tax[23] concession like an individual does. In New South Wales, an individual pays no land tax until their land is valued at more than $629,000. Property held in a Discretionary Trust receives no such concession and is therefore paying up to $10,164 more in land tax every year than an individual would pay. This is why we reiterate that trusts are not a one-size-fits-allsolution.

SUMMARY

A Discretionary Trust has many advantages but the investor needs to be mindful of the abovementioned pitfalls. Before delving into the other types of trusts available to the investor and business owner, there is a common confusion between companies and trusts that first needs to be explained—that is, how asset protection works ...

---

21 **incur:** make oneself subject to; bring upon oneself; become liable to.
22 **quarantined:** kept separate from something else by force; isolated.
23 **Land tax:** a tax on property imposed by states or territories; usually based on the estimated value of the property.

TAX FACTORS

- **There is no such thing as "one-size-fits-all" when it comes to structures. Each person's circumstances are different and need assessing before embarking on the use of structures.**

9

Asset Protection

THE DIFFERENCES BETWEEN COMPANIES AND TRUSTS

If you've eagerly turned straight to this chapter and haven't read the two previous chapters, we strongly recommend that you go back now and do so! It's essential to grasp the basics of both a company and a trust to understand the difference between them.

The need for asset protection is stronger than ever before and keeps becoming more prevalent in society. The Robin Hood mentality—"take from the rich"—fosters the rewarding of those who hold someone else responsible for their misfortune. This, in our opinion, is the definition of personal irresponsibility. We don't doubt for a second that there are special cases that do deserve reward, but with modern-day litigation, the principle has obviously been taken too far.

The end result when a society habitually assigns responsibility and blame to someone else is a society whose people dare not stick their neck out for anyone. Any attempt to help a fellow human being then has to be accompanied by a disclaimer, a legal document or even a live witness. And all in the name of protecting one's self while trying to help another. Addressing this social problem is not the purpose of this book, however.

Given that this Robin Hood mentality is persisting, it is sensible to ensure that you yourself are protected if you are in an industry prone to such litigation. Understanding asset protection can accomplish this. It starts with knowing the main difference between a trust and a company, which is:

▸ **Nobody owns a trust—it is *controlled*, not owned.**

A company is owned by shareholders and controlled by directors. A trust is owned by nobody and is controlled by the trustee. You can create a trust and control it but you will never own it. And this is a good thing.

This fundamental difference of ownership is how assets can be protected. Although you control the trust, nobody can take the assets from you because you don't own them.

Here's an example. If a house was purchased using a company structure, it would mean the company owns the asset. However, the company is split up into shares and, in turn, those shares are owned by individuals. The result is an *indirect* ownership.

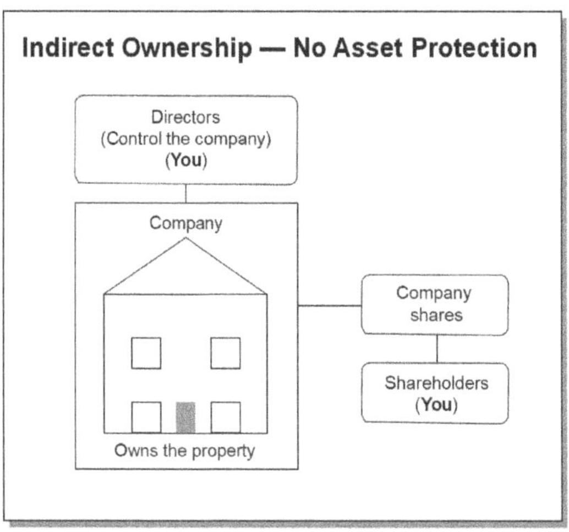

A share is considered an asset and can therefore be taken from the shareholder, if the shareholder is sued.

Purchasing a property using a trust is different. A trust owns the property—end of story. It is not owned by a human being; it is owned by the trust. The trustees can do what they please with the property: sell it, rent it out—whatever. Regardless of what action they take, all profits, income and money received from the property belong to the trust.

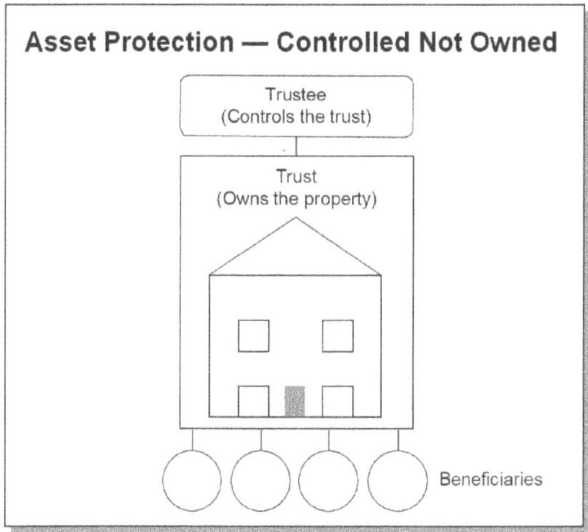

The trust owns the asset.

It's easy to see how asset protection is possible:

- **You own *nothing* and control everything.**

This concept often conflicts with the common dogma of society. Most people are trying to *own* everything: their home, car, etc. It is in fact not necessary to own things; control is far more important than ownership.

TRANSFERRING ASSETS INTO A TRUST

Usually when people realise that asset protection is achievable through trusts, their first inclination is to transfer everything they own into a trust. Unfortunately, it comes as quite a disappointment to realise that transferring assets into a trust comes with a price tag. For example, transferring property will incur the cost of stamp duty and possible capital gains tax. In essence, the act of transferring assets is considered similar to "selling" the asset and thus the same tax implications apply.

This brings us back to the Investing Sequence and why we advocate this fact:

- **The best time to set up asset protection is *before* you invest.**

However, don't feel too disheartened if you have lots of assets in your own name. You can do something about it. Depending on your situation there may be a way it can be done and our team might be able to help. One way that is possible for everyone is a method we call Equity Transfer, where over a period of several years you transfer your equity into a trust.

Here's how it works:

EQUITY TRANSFER

To grasp this concept you first need to realise what it is that you are trying to protect. Do you want asset protection to protect your house, investment property or car? The answer is no. What you are really trying to protect is the equity, the part you own, your capital. Sure, there may be sentimental value in your own home and with this method you can also protect that. However, you must first grasp that it's the equity you want to protect because it's the equity that someone else is after.

Here's an example. If you have several properties in your own name and want asset protection, you can borrow up to 80% (sometimes 90%) of the value of your assets. What do you do with this money? Well, you put it in a trust where you can buy more assets with it. The net result is the equity has been transferred into the trust. If someone were to come along and think, "Gee, Bill's got lots of property. He must be worth a million bucks ... I'll sue him!", they'll get a real shock when they discover that Bill is up to his eyeballs in debt. No solicitor would bother suing because there is nothing there to take.

If Bill had one million dollars worth of property with a total debt of $800,000, then after a fire sale[24] the liquidators might get $900,000 for properties worth a million; leaving only $100,000 when all loans are paid. It wouldn't be worth their hassle.

24 **fire sale:** sale of assets at very low prices, typically when the seller faces bankruptcy.

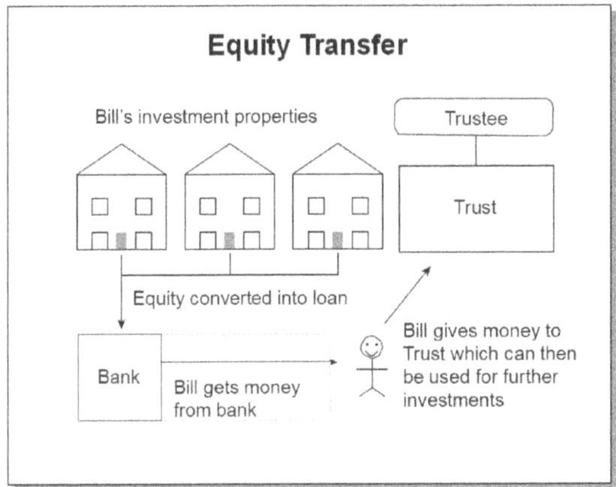

There are other methods of protecting the assets you have, but it requires a real understanding of your situation, using the services of an experienced accountant well versed in asset protection and structures. But this above example, while not the only option, gives you an idea of what is possible and an understanding that something can be done about it.

CONTRACTUAL WILL

Another useful method of protecting assets owned in your own name is through the use of a Contractual Will. Here's an example of how this works. Parents draw up a will stating that all properties are to be passed on to their son when they die. The parents enter into a contract with a trust, which then has various rights and obligations to their properties. Set up correctly, the trust now has priority over creditors and litigators who attempt to take the properties from the parents. While more costly than the Equity Transfer method, a Contractual Will is immediate.

SUMMARY

Asset protection is achieved through the use of trusts by separating control and ownership. It's important to note that your intentions for using the above methods or any other method of asset protection must be justifiable. It's a little late to try to protect your asset when you find yourself in the middle of a court battle or when creditors are knocking on your door. In fact, *any* method utilised whereby you are trying to avoid creditors or litigators can be undone. Asset protection and estate planning are done now for the future.

There are more trust structures you can use, which we will cover later, but regardless of your current situation, you now have the means and wherewithal to protect your assets and, by doing so, you will be able to pass on your wealth to future generations and have it protected from unnecessary fees, taxes and the Robin Hoods of this world.

TAX FACTORS

- **Nobody owns a trust—it is *controlled* not owned.**
- **You own *nothing* and control everything.**
- **The best time to set up asset protection is *before* you invest.**

10

Unit, Hybrid and Bare Trusts

Unit, Hybrid and Bare Trusts offer many advantages to the investor. The scope and utilisation of these entities extends far beyond the material covered in this chapter and we recommend that you consult a professional before establishing any type of structure. For more information visit www.chan-naylor.com.au

UNIT TRUST

A unit is a portion of the trust which gives the holder the right to profits. Profits and income are distributed via the units to the individual. Beneficial ownership is determined by the amount of units held by a person. Units can be sold to other people, entitling them to the profits of the trust. Unit Trusts are very useful, especially for investors, because different types of units can be issued.

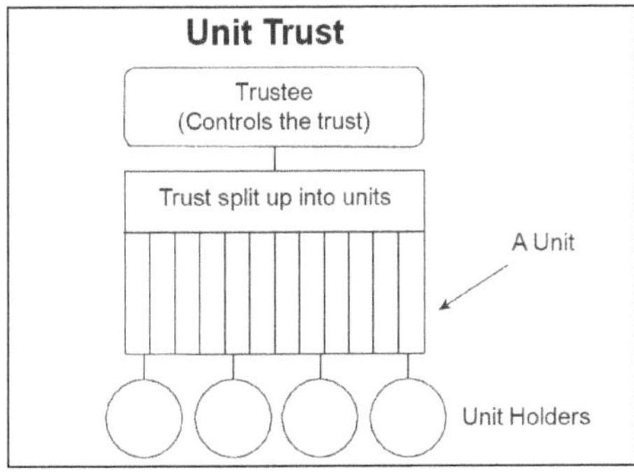

The units can be defined as:

a. Income Units—entitles the holder to income only.

b. Capital Units—entitles the holder to capital only.

c. Ordinary Units—entitles the holder to both income and capital.

Therefore, if a Unit Trust is receiving income, such as rent, from a property investment, the income is diverted to the income unit holder. The figure below demonstrates this example.

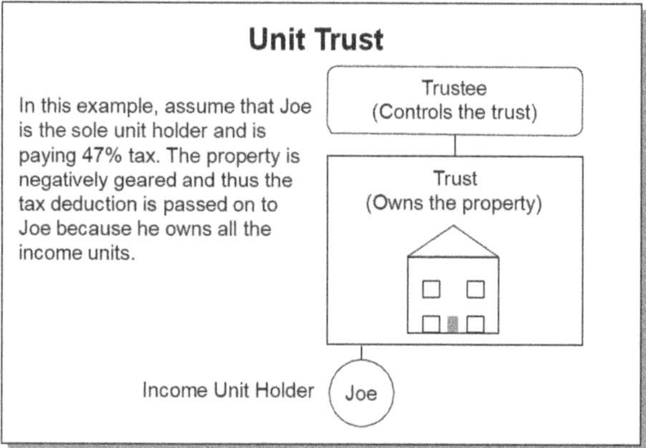

Note: The example above does not take into account the possible capital gains tax issues if and when Joe decides to redeem his units.

HYBRID TRUST

As mentioned, a Hybrid Trust is a cross between a Discretionary and a Unit Trust. This type of structure is quite appealing because it includes the benefits of both and is an extremely useful structure. You can split the trust up into units while also having beneficiaries to distribute to at your discretion.

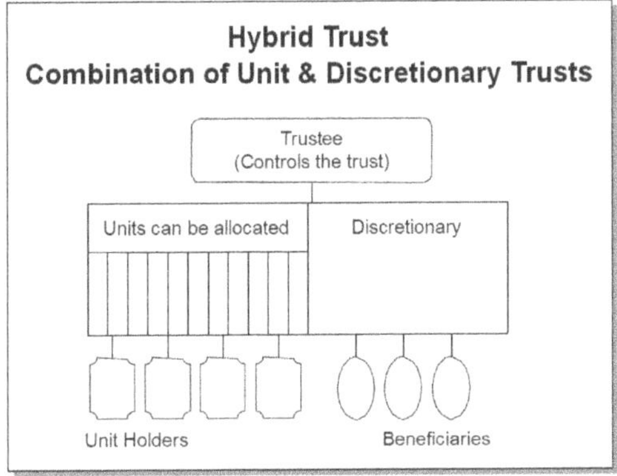

When borrowing, a Hybrid Trust offers the most flexibility and is particularly useful between non-related parties, because you can fix entitlements while also maintaining discretion. Asset protection is also possible— capital can be owned by another trust.

BARE TRUST

A Bare Trust is also known as Declaration of Trust and is a useful structure when ownership privacy is a concern.

As you know, a trust separates ownership and control, with the beneficiaries (or unit holders) entitled to the profits and assets of a trust. A Bare Trust, however, reverses the roles to a degree because the beneficiary of a Bare Trust has control over the trustee. With a Bare Trust, the trustee follows the direction of the beneficiary. To the world, the asset may look as though it belongs to the trustee because the trustee's name is on all legal documents and the trustee *appears* to have legal control. However, per the deed of a Bare Trust, the beneficiary can, at any time, instruct the trustee to transfer the assets into the beneficiary's name.

Unlike other types of trusts, the trustee of a Bare Trust is not required to do anything with the asset. The trustee just holds the asset and must do whatever the beneficiary says regarding the asset. When the beneficiaries want the asset "back" they simply ask for it back.

As you may be wondering under what circumstance you would use a Bare Trust, here are some examples.

Your next-door neighbour recently put his home up for sale and you want to buy it, so you can knock it down and build a tennis court. It is, after all, the oldest and most unkempt house in the whole street. Unfortunately, when you mention your wonderful plan, he flies off the handle and raves on about the sentimental value of his home. You try to reason with him, but he is now bound and determined to never let *you* buy it. So what you do is ask your friend to be the trustee of a Bare Trust and you tell your friend to go and buy the house next door on your behalf, secretly. After the sale is complete, you then exercise your right as beneficiary of the Bare Trust and have the property transferred into your name. There is nominal stamp duty and no capital gains tax when you transfer the property from your trustee's name to your name, in this example. You now own the property and your ex-neighbour is none the wiser.

Another example is if you want to be a major shareholder in a new company, but don't wish to have your name on the share register for the time being. In this circumstance, you can use a Bare Trust and have the trustee buy the shares. Only the trustee's name will appear on the share register and you can exercise your right under the deed whenever you choose.

A Bare Trust is a great tool for using other people to act on your behalf; it almost allows you to be in two places at once! Therefore, a Bare Trust protects your money, the assets and your identity all at the same time.

SUMMARY

The trick to using trusts is forward planning. You should really have a good idea of what you will be investing in, the amount of money you will be making and when the profits are likely to be received. And you should consult with your accountant *before* entering into a transaction and *before* the end of the financial year to ensure that you have everything in order. (Yes, it's that Investor Sequence rule again—very important!)

11

Deceased Estates and Divorce

You could say this is the most depressing chapter of the book. While we don't want to concentrate on negative subjects such as death or divorce, for the investor and business owner, they are part and parcel of life. You might have heard it said that there are two things you can be certain of in life—one is death and the other is taxes. We are only able to help you with one of them! However, while such things can cause tremendous heartache and misery, we hope that by sharing the information contained in this chapter the financial burdens will be somewhat lessened. Quite often, the financial consequences of death or divorce are not realised until afterwards, often causing further emotional upset which may have been avoided had this information been known.

TESTAMENTARY TRUSTS

It's a sad fact that someday we all die. We hate to be blunt, but it is true. Family bickering over who gets what, unfortunate as it may seem, does occur. In severe cases where family feuds result in the assets being sold to evenly distribute the wealth, unnecessary tax implications dilute the value of the estate considerably.

One of the definitions of "testament" is a legal document declaring a person's wishes regarding the disposal of their assets when they die. Therefore, a Testamentary Trust is a trust set up based on the direction of a will (of the deceased) and is similar in nature to a Discretionary Trust.

What happens is that after death the will is activated and the Testamentary Trust is established. All assets are transferred into the trust based on the direction of the will. No stamp duty or taxes are incurred under this arrangement.

The result is immediate asset protection for the surviving beneficiaries. And one of the greatest benefits is that minors (those under 18 years of age) are not penalised for receiving income from such a trust. You may recall that if a minor receives income from a trust and the income is not related to personal exertion (they did not work for the money), then the tax rate is 66% for amounts between $416 and $1307 with 47% tax paid for amounts above $1307. However, under a Testamentary Trust, the adult tax rates apply, allowing them to earn $18,200 (or $20,500 with low income tax offset) tax free every year.

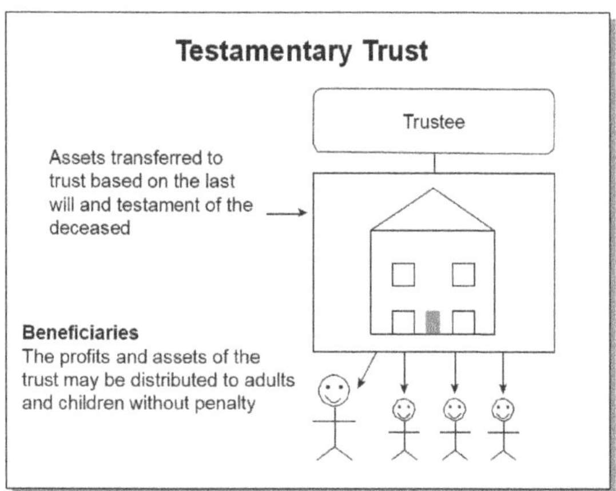

CAPITAL VESTED TRUSTS

Vested is something that is fixed and cannot be changed by anyone. A Capital Vested Trust protects the capital by separating the rights to the capital from the rights to income by allowing the trustee access to the income only. If a person received property from a deceased estate where the deceased made no plan to use a Testamentary Trust, the asset would end up in the recipient's name. Having it in their own name, of course, provides no asset protection and any income received by that person would be taxed at their marginal rate.[25]

25 **marginal rate:** the increasing tax rate paid on income as it rises. See Income Tax Rates Table in Chapter 5.

In the absence of a Testamentary Trust, anyone receiving assets from a deceased estate can have the assets transferred into a Capital Vested Trust. This must be done within three years from the date of death of the owner of the deceased estate. The benefits of doing so are asset protection, reduction of CGT and income distribution. Also, as is the case with Testamentary Trusts, minors can receive income and capital from the trust without penalty.

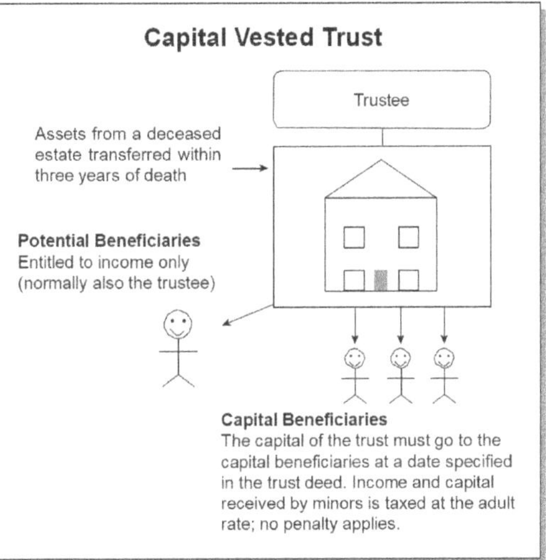

The rules for such a trust are that the capital can only go to the capital beneficiaries and anyone who is acting as trustee is only entitled to income. Therefore, in the case of a mother of three children whose spouse has passed away, the mother would be the trustee and entitled to income, while the children would be capital beneficiaries and entitled to both income and capital.

CHILD MAINTENANCE TRUSTS

Divorce is a touchy subject especially when children are involved, as they often are. It can be a rather messy situation. In the fight about who gets what, the maintenance of the children is a major consideration. Often what is not considered is asset protection and the tax implications of splitting and selling the assets.

There is, however, a structure available that protects the assets and income for the benefit of the children.

The Child Maintenance Trust is pretty much the same as a Capital Vested Trust. Upon a marriage breakdown the assets can be transferred into a Child Maintenance Trust, protecting the assets for the children's future. And as with a Capital Vested Trust, children under the age of 18 receiving income are taxed at adult rates.

Therefore, if a joint agreement can be reached between the divorcing parties, the set-up of such a structure can be arranged which, under the circumstances, provides the best possible financial solution for the children and protects the assets from whatever else the parents might get up to next!

SUMMARY

Therefore, in the case of death or divorce, as tough as it may seem, if you plan for the future you can possibly make it a little better for all those involved.

12

The Trust Guide

Now that you've learned quite a bit about the different types of trusts and how they can be used to protect assets while subsequently lessening the individual tax burden, we thought we'd summarised what you've learned in an easy guide for future reference.

Following is the Trust Guide, a table that identifies the advantages and disadvantages of using certain trusts. It is not intended to be a comprehensive description of what is possible with each trust. Rather, the purpose of the Trust Guide is to outline, at a simple glance, the possible pitfalls in using certain trusts as well as the advantages.

In reviewing this table, you'll notice several trusts that have not yet been explained. Below is a brief description of these.

FAMILY TRUST

A Family Trust is almost the same as a Discretionary Trust with the exception that beneficiaries are restricted to family members.

PROPERTY INVESTOR TRUST™ DEED

This is a combination trust especially set up for the benefit of property investors. It utilises the benefits of Unit Trusts and Hybrid Trusts and overcomes problems associated with asset protection and land tax issues, while maintaining flexibility between the distribution of income and capital.

Trust Guide Table

	Company	Family Trust	Discretionary Trust	Unit Trust	Hybrid Trust	Bare Trust	Testamentary Trust	Capital Vested Trust	Child Maintenance Trust	Property Investor Trust™	Self-Managed Super Fund
General											
Tax rate	30%/ 27.5% (SME)	I	I	I	I	I	I	I	I	I	15%
Advantages											
Asset protection		•	•	•	•	•	•	•	•	•	•
Negative gearing claimable by beneficiary or unit holder				•	•	•				•	
Minors entitled to income without tax penalty							•	•	•		
Possible land tax concession available	•			•			•	•	•	•	•
Profits distribution at trustee's choice		•	•		•					•	
Disadvantages											
No asset protection if set up incorrectly	•			•		•					
Losses quarantined	•	•	•				•	•	•		•
Minors penalised		•	•	•	•	•				•	
Income & capital distribution determined by deed (not necessarily disadvantage)				•	•		•	•	•	•	•

I: The individual rate paid by the person receiving the income.

Please note: The company structure has been included for comparison against trusts.

13

The Property Investor Trust™ Deed

Since the release of the first edition of this book, many readers have requested further explanation of

the Property Investor Trust™ Deed, affectionately called the PIT™. We've included this chapter for the purpose of answering those commonly asked questions.

In order to understand why the PIT was developed, it's important to know a little of how our legal system operates. When there is a difference of opinion between a company and the ATO, or an individual and the ATO,such cases end up in court. It's the Commissioner versus John Doe or the Commissioner versus a corporation.

The opposing views are resolved by a judge. It's the judge who interprets the law and decides who is right.

What often becomes a deciding point in these cases is the *exact* definition of certain words. That's why there are specific definitions for words in the tax law, because they may differ from their normal usage.

Trust deeds are written differently by different lawyers. They are generally written to be broad and general, covering many purposes. They are written in a way that gives the trustee broad powers. The potential problem with this is that such broad powers are then open to interpretation and opinion.

Rather than have a deed which is broad and generic in its description of what it can do, the PIT deed is designed to be very specific. The PIT describes the powers of the trustee in a very specific area–property! It encompasses property developing, renovations, joint ventures and, of course, the ability to buy and sell property. It does not allow the trustee to buy shares or run a business through the trust.

While the PIT is similar to a Hybrid Trust, it has been specifically designed for property investors, and also has other advantages.

TRUSTS DO NOT LAST FOREVER

The other flaw with trusts is the fact that they do not last forever.

Typically, a trust must vest[26] in 80 years. This means the assets of a trust are passed on to the beneficiaries at the time of vesting. The potential downside to this is stamp duty and capital gains tax costs for the receiving beneficiaries. Also, asset protection is no longer possible if the individual owns the asset.

Having spent many months researching this point, and with the help of tax lawyers, a trust was created that has no vesting date. For some this may not be an issue because they figure, "Well, I'm not here so why worry about it!" However, our purpose is to increase and protect the net worth of business owners and investors and we endeavour to do it from generation to generation. Therefore, we believe it was necessary to find a solution and provide a deed that did not vest. This is another benefit of the PIT.

HOW TO CLAIM INTEREST WHEN USING A TRUST

One of the main pitfalls that investors fall into is using a trust that doesn't allow for negative gearing of investments. As we have mentioned, Discretionary Trusts (for example) quarantine the losses. This means the losses get trapped inside the trust and the individual is unable to claim those losses against his or her income. The result is that negative gearing cannot be achieved.

When you borrow money that is used for investing purposes, the interest on that loan is tax deductible for investors. This is common knowledge. This principle is utilised in the establishment of a trust.

First, the investor borrows money from a bank. That money is then used to buy units in a trust (with the intention of receiving a commercial benefit as the

26 **vest:** to place property or power in the control of another person or group.

property generates a positive return over time). The trust now has a lump sum which it uses to buy a property. The property is then owned by the trust and the individual has financed the investment and is able to claim the interest as a tax deduction against their personal income. The rent is received as income and the trust pays for expenses out of the rent received (that is, agents' fees, water rates etc). What usually makes a property negatively geared is the interest on the loan, as the rental income often covers the outgoings associated with owning an investment property. Keep in mind, however, that if the trust makes a loss (it cannot cover its own expenses) then that loss remains in the trust. Neither the beneficiary nor the trustee can claim that loss personally. When the trust makes a profit, that loss is then taken into account.

In addition to using a Property Investor Trust™ Deed, the above can also be achieved with a Unit or Hybrid Trust. However the ATO has issued Tax Determination TD 2009/17 and is basically against using Hybrid Trusts as Hybrid Trust Deeds are different from author to author. We do not use Unit Trusts for property as a rule because it triggers an E4 Capital Gain Tax problem effectively increasing the capital gain tax upon the sale of the property and redemption of units. The Property Investor Trust Deed™ was created by Chan & Naylor specifically for property investing and has an ATO Approved Product Ruling PR2014/15, PR2011/15, and PR2018/6. Refer to https://www.chan-naylor.com.au/trust-not-trust-property-investments/ for the benefits of using a PIT™ for property investing. Due to the fact that a Discretionary Trust doesn't have provisions for issuing units, it cannot be done using this form of trust.

When establishing a trust, whether it's a PIT or any other type of trust, the individual must be certain of their intentions. This is part of the Investor Sequence™— you must have your investment plan in place. This is imperative, not just to ensure that you are establishing the right structure, but to also ensure that you are using it correctly as time goes by.

The PIT, like any other trust, is not for everybody. Each person's circumstances still need to be addressed before setting up any type of structure. You can find more information about the PIT by visiting www.chan-naylor. com.au.

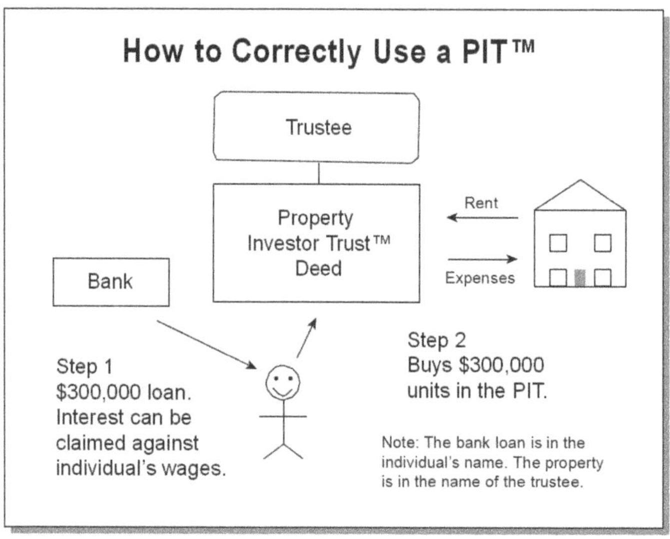

ATO RULINGS AND UPDATES

The ATO has issued several rulings and statements that further explain the correct use of trusts and the treatment of units. The reader can get more information from the ATO website (www.ato.gov.au) by searching their legal database online. The tax ruling that specifically relates to units is *IT 2684: Deductibility of Interest on Money Borrowed to Acquire Units in a Property Unit Trust.* The reader is advised to read this ruling which can be found by searching the online legal database for "IT 2684".

Prior to releasing TD 2009/17 the following were released:

1. Tax Alert TA 2008/3 plus media release 2008/13, issued 26 March 2008.

2. Draft Tax Determination TD 2008/D16, issued 19 November 2008.

3. Compendium TD 2009/17EC in response to matters raised re TD 2008/D16.

4. Tax Determination TD 2009/17, issued 15 July 2009.

This can also be found on the ATO legal database and is worth reading. As a brief summary for readers, the ATO have now stipulated the following:

In order to claim interest on money borrowed to purchase units in a trust these requirements must be met:

1. There must be commerciality, which means thatwhen investing you must have an intention to make a profit either in the short or long term and you are not entering into a tax avoidance scheme.

2. The investor has a directed and fixed entitlement to income and capital from the trust in proportion to the investment made and the trustee does not have the power to change what would be a fixed entitlement.

3. There is no benefit that will be offered to others via the trust regarding this investment.

4. If the taxpayer only gets a portion of the benefits, such as the income only, but receives none of the capital benefits, then they can only claim a portion of their expenses, including their interest on their loans.

Around February 2010 in *Forrest v. ATO,* Andrew Forrest won a Full Federal Court case against the ATO where the Court stated that one may buy income only units in a Hybrid trust and provided there was fixed entitlement to the income, the interest was fully tax deductible on the loan acquired to purchase these income only units.

The ATO did not have a chance to put forward their apportionment argument as the years under consideration were before the ATO Tax Determination TD 2009/17. In an ATO Practice Statement on this issue they advise that they will require apportionment if the tax payer does not have a fixed entitlement to all the income and capital.

According to ITR 2684, as long as the unit holder has both an income and capital entitlement then the interest on the loan is fully deductible.

In the Property Investors Trust Deed, ordinary units are issued which entitle the unit holder to a fixed entitlement of both capital and income and hence the interest on the loan is fully deductible. As per ITR 2684, TD 2009/17 and *Forrest v. ATO.*

Some may say that if you are issuing both capital and income to the unit holder, the unit holder will lose their asset protection benefits because the capital component of the units is an asset and can be claimed by a creditor.

In most Hybrid or Unit Trust Deeds this is true because the creditor can force the unit holder to liquidate its ownership of the units and the creditor can now get access to the cash.

However in the PIT, the deed is drafted in such a way that the creditor cannot force the unit holder to liquidate their units.

The only way units can be liquidated is if the trustee redeems the units. Hence we not only afford our unit holders withasset protection but the deed has no vesting date and thereis a lineage clause which protects the assets within theblood line if the trust is forcibly dismantled.

As we have already mentioned, the rules are constantly changing and a Player needs to keep up to date with these changes. One simple way is to subscribe to the ATO Taxpayers' Alerts. You can do this via www.ato.gov.au/atp. This is a great service that provides information about unauthorised tax schemes, dodgy investments, special checklists for investors and new rulings mentioned above— all of which are very worthwhile to know about *before* youinvest your money!

Note: For more information on the Property Investor Trust™ refer to https://www.chan-naylor.com.au/trust-not-trust-property-investments/

Chan & Naylor developed the Property Investor Trust™ (PIT™) and has a Registered Trade Mark on both the name and the structure.

The Property Investor Trust™ (PIT™) also has an approved Product Ruling from the ATO PR2014/15 and PR2011/15.

14

Understanding Property and Negative Gearing

Property is, for the most part and certainly for the long term, a wonderful investment. There are many facets of property investing, including developing or renovating for either commercial or residential markets. One can even venture into resort or holiday investment properties whereby you're adding a service to enhance the income while still benefiting from capital growth.

Although all these methods of property investing have made many people wealthy, this chapter is dedicated to the residential property investment market. You'll find, however, that many of the rules apply to all property investing styles.

In Australia, the price of residential real estate has enjoyed continued and consistent growth for over 150 years. Apart from other economic factors such as a growing population or additional infrastructure, one of the major modern day contributing factors is the tax benefit investors receive for owning investment property.

Many investors, to their undoubted delight, have suddenly discovered their net worth to be in excess of a million dollars—all because their accountant told them to buy a couple of properties to reduce tax!

GEARING EXPLAINED

Gearing, in the financial context, is achieving more with less. It can be likened to the gears on a bicycle. The bigger gear is linked by a chain to a smaller gear. When the rider turns the pedal one full revolution this turns the smaller gear twice. The result is twice the reward: twice the speed and twice the distance. Bicycles with many gears allow the rider greater speeds, with the similar effort of turning the pedals one full revolution.

And so it is with investing. The money you put in is increased by gearing, which increases the speed of your wealth creation. The less money you put into a deal the more you are geared and the greater the return. A Player tries as hard as they can to put nothing in by borrowing 100%—and as long as the investment grows, the percentage ROI is infinity!

Negative gearing is where the rental doesn't quite cover the property expenses such as loan payments and maintenance, so you have to put in some of your own money. Neutral gearing is where income and expenses are equal; the property pays for itself. Lastly, positive gearing is where you are making an income from the property after all expenses are paid.

In the late eighties and throughout the nineties, negative gearing became almost a fad. It was the most common answer to lessening the tax bill. In recent times, the idea of losing money on a property has been shunned, namely by visiting American wealth gurus. They (and rightly so) can't understand why someone would invest to lose money. Their dogma is "focus on income" or "cash flow" and so the tide is changing with more investors seeking a positively geared property.

What should a property investor do? Negatively gear a property or follow the American wisdom and buy only positively geared property? Our opinion is this. One rule already mentioned in this book is:

▶ **Never invest purely for a tax deduction. Never.**

An investment *must* provide a return—it must have an ROI (Return *of* and Return *on* the Investment). Given this fact, a tax benefit is a bonus.

When you take a look at residential property investment, you can't go past the fact that investors have made money! Despite the investment costing $50 or $100 per week.

Although we agree with our American comrades that being negatively geared should be avoided, you have to remember that we live in a different country with different tax laws.

For example, in the USA you get a tax deduction on your own home. That's their way of encouraging home ownership. Here in Australia, the government encourages investing by offering a tax benefit on investment properties.

Furthermore, the economic environment in the USA is not the same as here; finance works differently and the real estate market is very different.

Here in Australia, rental returns often aren't enough to cover the loan costs so the owner has to chip in (negative gearing). Deciding on the type of property is best answered by those with property *investing* experience and is not the purpose of this book. The main point is, don't ever purposely keep a property negatively geared to save tax— that's a one-sided look at a two-sided equation. If you're paying more tax it's because you're making more money! Remember that.

PROPERTY OWNERSHIP

Ownership is an important factor to consider when purchasing an investment property. We've seen many people disheartened when they realise that not all deductions are available to them because of the ownership arrangement.

Rule:

- **When property ownership is shared, your tax deductions are also shared.**

What tends to happen is that a couple will purchase a property together and split the ownership 50/50. Although a sign of their faithfulness and love, it can affect the tax benefits.

Example:

Mr and Mrs Jones own 50% each of an investment property. If the total expenses for the year were $20,000 then they each can claim a $10,000 tax deduction. Let's say hubby is on a salary earning $170,000 and the wife earns nothing because she is working full time looking after the newborn.

	Husband	Wife
Annual Income	$200,000	Nil
Property Ownership	50%	50%
Tax Deductions from Property	$10,000	$10,000
Taxable Income	$190,000	Nil
Tax Rate	47%	0%
Tax Saving	$4700	Nil
Total Saving	$4700	Nil

You can see that the wife's $10,000 tax deduction is wasted. What if the property was 100% owned by the hubby?

	Husband
Annual Income	$200,000
Property Ownership	100%
Tax Deductions from Property	$20,000
Taxable Income	$180,000
Tax Rate	47%
Tax Saving	$9400
Total Saving	$9400

There you have it—an extra $4700 (for that tax year) just from a difference in ownership. Based on this example, that's an extra $90 per week which may well turn a negatively geared property into a neutrally geared one.

Please note that this is just an example and not a recommendation that property should be owned by the highest income earner. In fact, we don't recommend this at all because it can lead to future tax and asset protection issues.

Ownership of an investment is critical and the most common ownership mistake we find is this:

- When property is personally owned and it is negatively geared, the person with the biggest salary takes majority ownership.

This is only of benefit while the property is negatively geared. Once, over time, the property becomes positively geared, the income will be received by the highest income earner. Therefore, the income is likely to be taxed at 47%. This problem can be overcome with the use of the right structure.

The overall Tax Factor for ownership when investing is this:

► Investor ownership must be decided before purchase.

LAND TAX

This may also affect the ownership decision. Land tax is a state level tax and therefore is different from state to state. The implications of it, however, are far reaching and uninformed investors may find themselves paying more than they need to. This subject is covered in the next chapter.

ASSET PROTECTION

Another implication to consider in regards to ownership is the susceptibility each person has to being sued. If the higher income earner is in a profession that is highly litigable,[27] then the assets might be better protected through a trust. Again, such matters involve numerous factors and require at least a general knowledge of what is possible and the advantages and disadvantages of the different vehicles available.

LONG TERM OR SHORT TERM?

Your investment strategy can also affect ownership. If the property is to be sold (rather than held on to) then majority ownership in the name of the lower income earner may be more beneficial. From Chapter 5, you'll remember that your income tax rate determines your capital gain tax rate (the lower the income tax, the less capital gains tax). Therefore, if your investment strategy is a quick buy and sell, resulting (hopefully) in a nice capital profit, then consider the lower income earner as the majority owner to reduce CGT.

27 **litigable:** giving cause for lawsuit; able to be pursued in court.

If your strategy is more long-term and you plan to hold on to the property for some time, then in addition to the above Tax Factor, you need to know that:

- ▶**Asset protection and your investment strategy are deciding factors of property ownership.**

HOW DEPRECIATION MAKES YOU MONEY

Depreciation is the value that an asset loses over time. The opposite is appreciation—the amount that an assetincreases over time.

We all know that property goes up in value. The strange thing is that you can claim depreciation on the building. The basic assumption is that the building and its fixtures[28] and fittings[29] are losing value as they get older. This is true enough too; an old house is generally less appealing than a new one. The government has set the average life of a house to be 40 years. This means that you depreciate the value of the house over a 40-year period, which equates to 2.5% per year. So every year, 2.5% of the value of the building is claimable as a tax deduction against your income!

This type of tax deduction is called a non-cash deduction and is very important to the investor because you're getting a tax deduction without spending any money! (Alleluia!) For example, if the building is said to be worth $200,000 then you'll get a $5000 tax deduction each year ($200,000 x 2.5% = $5000). Remember, this doesn't include the land so the total value of the whole property might be $800,000 if the land was worth $600,000.

How do you use depreciation? First, you need to value the building, fixtures and fittings and to do this most people employ the skills of a quantity surveyor. This person's sole task is to provide a written report on the value of the building, fixtures and fittings. The report is often called a Depreciation Schedule which is used by your accountant to work out your tax deductions. This depreciation rule of 2.5% applies only to properties built after September

28 **fixtures:** in real estate, a piece of the property that is permanently attached. The fixture is considered a part of the property if it shares the same useful life as the rest of the property. Example: kitchen cupboards.

29 **fittings:** furnishings; items that are added that could be removed. Example: lights or curtain rails.

1985. Therefore, newer property has more depreciation value than older property because property 20 years old has already been depreciated at 2.5% for the past 20 years.

Using a Depreciation Schedule, you receive a tax deduction even though you haven't spent the money. Unlike claiming the expense associated with buying a new oven where you first need to spend money to get a tax deduction, a Depreciation Schedule allows you to claim against the loss of value of the building—without you spending any money.

Let's say you just bought the property, then hire a quantity surveyor immediately and get a Depreciation Schedule from them. You've spent no money on the property at all (other than buying it) yet you can claim depreciation at 2.5% of the total value of the property, every year, until the property is 40 years old.

In our experience many property investors are missing out on thousands of dollars of tax deductions by not using a Depreciation Schedule. If you fit into this category,don't worry because you can still claim the last four years worth of depreciation if you haven't. One lady, as you'llsee in our real life examples, was able to claim four years worth of depreciation that her previous accountant had failed to claim and got a whopping $50,000 tax deduction giving her a $25,000 (approximate) tax refund!

One last bit of advice on this: don't allow your accountant to provide you with a Depreciation Schedule. We recommend that you use Quantity Surveyor who will actuallygo out and visit the property. With new properties, sometimes the builder provides a Depreciation Schedule which canbe used.

▸**A Depreciation Schedule should always be used for investment properties built after September 1985.**

Note: Change to the law means from 1st July 2017 depreciation on old plant & equipment can no longer be claimed when you have incurred the expense.

MAXIMISING YOUR PROPERTY TAX DEDUCTIONS

When you spend the money and *what* you spend it on determines whether the expense is offset against income or capital gain. To understand how to go about it correctly and remain legal, it is necessary to understand both the definitions of the following terms and what their tax implications are.

Any expense incurred in owning an investment property fits into one of four categories.

1. Outgoings
2. Repairs and Maintenance
3. Plant[30] and Equipment
4. Capital Improvements

How much you can claim as a deduction depends on which of the above four categories an expense falls into.

DEFINITIONS

Outgoings—these are your normal, regular expenses associated with owning property such as water rates, council rates, strata levies, interest on loans etc. Outgoings are 100% tax deductible against income.

Repairs & Maintenance—replacement or renewal of broken or worn-out parts caused by tenants or damage. Repairs & Maintenance are 100% tax deductible against income.

Plant & Equipment—replacing an item such as carpet, a stove, a hot water service etc. Plant & Equipment depreciation is tax deductible against income. Depreciation is calculated at a specified rate depending on the item's expected lifetime.

Capital Improvements—replacement of an entire structure or unit of property (such as a whole new kitchen) is classed as a Capital Improvement. Capital Improvements are added to Cost Base and depreciated at 2.5% for 40 years which can be claimed as a tax deduction. This deduction is called the Special Building Write-off.

30 **plant:** the equipment and machinery necessary for carrying on a business. For the property investor it relates to such things as dishwashers, ovens, etc.

Cost Base—the total cost of the property. Any Capital Improvements are added to the Cost Base.

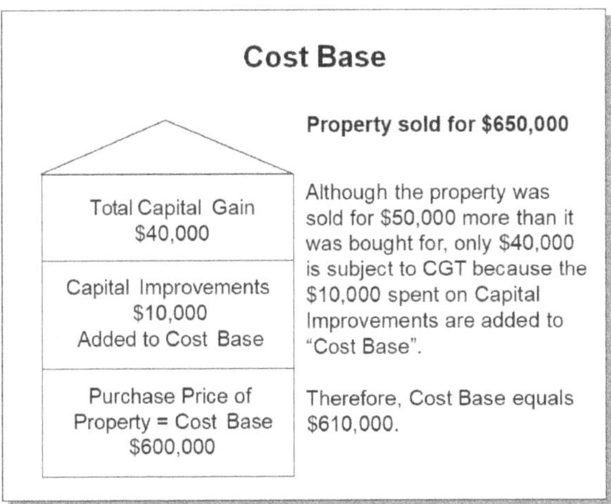

REPAIRS AND RENOVATIONS

Many investors believe that if they buy a property and "do it up", the money spent will be 100% deductible against their income. This is not the case.

When money is spent on repairs and renovations of an investment property, for it to be classed as an expense (100% deductible against income), you must be able to answer yes to the following two questions:

1. Is it a normal outgoing expense or a repair (a replacement or renewal of a broken or worn-out part caused by tenants or damage)?

2. Has the property been tenanted *or* is the property available for rent?

If you can answer yes then great, it is 100% deductible against your income. If you answered no to either question then the amount you spend is added to the Cost Base, which means that when you sell the property you'll pay less CGT. However, for those of you who don't sell (accumulating as many houses as possible and holding on to them), you need to plan ahead in order to maximise your tax deductions.

No matter what, *any* legitimate expense you incur with your investment property is either immediately claimable or added to the Cost Base. Failure to do otherwise is throwing money away!

- **Any legitimate expense associated with your investment falls into one of two categories:**

1. Claimed as an income expense (100% deductible or depreciated over time).
2. Claimed as a capital expense when the investment is sold.

The following diagrams give you a guideline as to what is considered a repair or renovation. While other factors may need to be considered, this should clear up any common misunderstandings.

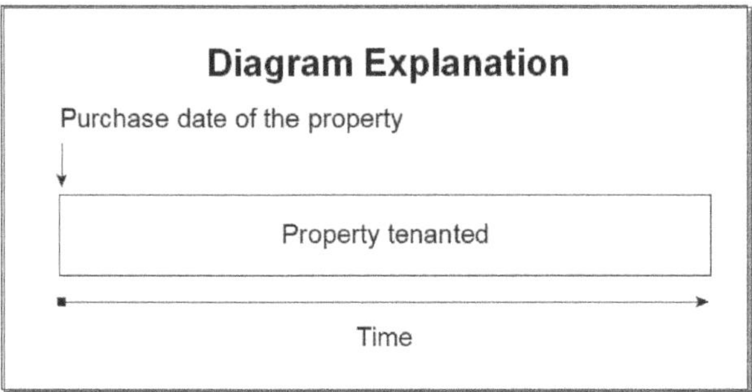

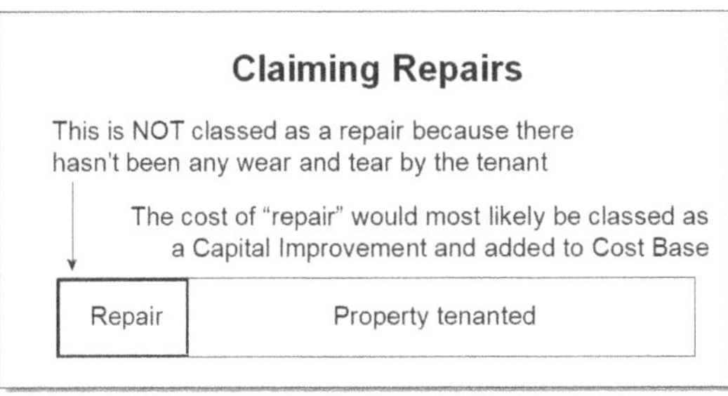

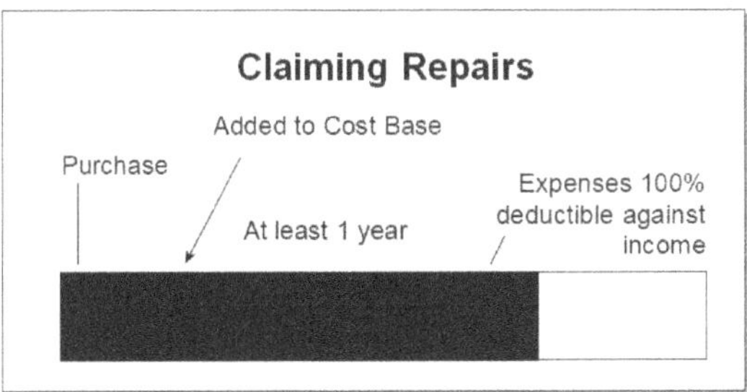

CLAIMING TRAVEL AS A PROPERTY INVESTOR

From 1st July 2017 travel expenses relating to inspecting, maintaining or collecting rent for a residential rental property cannot be claimed as deduction by investor. The travel expenditure is also not recognised in the cost base of the property for capital gains tax purpose.

HOW SALARY EARNERS CAN INCREASE THEIR INCOME

If you're on a salary, instead of waiting until the end of the financial year to get your tax return, you can submit a special form that entitles you to receive your tax deductions with every pay cheque.

For example, assume that over a year all the expenses relating to your property total $10,000 net of the rent received. This is a tax deduction that is taken off your gross income. If you're in the highest tax bracket, you then get a tax refund of $4,700 at the end of the financial year.

By completing a special form, you can get that $4,700 of tax put back in your pay cheque. That means your weekly income amount would go up by about $90. If you get paid fortnightly, it would increase by $180 and if you get paid monthly then your pay would increase by $391 per month. All that is happening is that you're paying less tax, but what's the point of giving it to the government only to ask for it back? You may as well adjust your tax rate and keep the money in your back pocket.

This special form is known by several names. It's most popular name was the 221D; more recently it's been called the Tax Variation Form. Most licensed tax agents are well versed in these. What you're basically doing is submitting a mini tax return.

Keep in mind that you do have to submit this every year to get the benefit. You can do more than one per year if necessary; that is, if you acquire another investment property during the financial year.

Completing a Tax Variation Form has helped many people ease the reduced cash flow of negative gearing and, for some, it has meant the difference between being able to afford an investment property and not being able to afford one.

If you currently own investments (such as property) that are reducing your cash flow and you haven't yet submitted a Tax Variation Form, then contact your accountant or visit www.chan-naylor.com.au for more information on how to do it.

RECORD KEEPING

You need to keep records of both income and expenses relating to your rental property for five years from the date you lodge your tax return.

For capital gains tax purposes, you must start keeping records when you purchase or make improvements to the property.

You must keep records relating to ownership and all the costs of assets for five years from the date you sell them.

You must keep records which set out:

- **The date you purchased the asset.**
- **The date you sold the asset and anything received in exchange.**

- **Any amount that would form part of the cost base of the asset.**

Do not send these records in with your tax return. Keep them in case the ATO asks to see them.

TAX FACTORS

- **Never invest purely for a tax deduction. Never.**
- **When property ownership is shared, your tax deductions are also shared.**
- **Investor ownership must be decided before purchase.**
- **Asset protection and your investment strategy are deciding factors of property ownership.**
- **A Depreciation Schedule should always be used for investment properties built after September 1985.**
- **Any legitimate expense associated with your investment falls into one of two categories:**

    1. Claimed as an income expense (100% deductible or depreciated over time).

    2. Claimed as a capital expense when the investment is sold.

15

Land Tax

Property investors around Australia need to be aware of the implications of land tax. Being a state tax, it differs from state to state; however, there are some basics you should consider.

One of the most misunderstood rules about land tax is who is responsible for paying it. Believe it or not, it comes down to a single date and time. States have different dates, so we'll call it the Deciding Date. The owner of the property at midnight on the Deciding Date is responsible for paying the land tax for the *next* year. The table on the next page shows what the Deciding Dates are for each state.

Another pitfall is that land tax thresholds[31] can be "lost". If hubby and wife own a property together, you would assume that the individual thresholds are added together, allowing the couple to claim a combined land tax threshold. However, in New South Wales if a couple owns an investment property 50/50 with a land value of $500,000 they can only claim a $629,000 threshold, not a combined threshold of $1,258,000. Furthermore, they have both used their $629,000 threshold on the one property. Some states are different and allow the land value to be split between the owners.

The investor must also consider the implications of using trusts to buy property. Trusts are treated differently in each state and the land tax rate can depend on the type of trust you use. For example, Queensland has a threshold for trusts, whereas New South Wales doesn't.

31 **Land tax threshold:** the amount of land that can be held free of land tax. It is different from state to state.

Surprisingly, the most complex land tax legislation is in the smallest place, the Australian Capital Territory. For these reasons we've left it out of the table. You can, however, visit www.revenue.act.gov.au for more information.

You'll also notice that the Northern Territory is not included in the table because they don't have any land tax legislation and you never, never know, it's likely they never, never will!

As the land value increases, so too does the tax rate. The following table shows only the initial threshold and the first level of land tax rates. Also keep in mind that the thresholds change every year. Visit the applicable state government website for more information on their land tax rates.

▸ **Property ownership affects land tax.**

NSW Land tax 2018

Threshold	Rate
$629,000	$100 plus 1.6% up to premium threshold.

Premium Threshold	Rate
$3,846,000	$51,572 for the first $3,846,000 then 2% over that.

Victoria — Land tax general rates 2009 — present

Total taxable value of land holdings	Land tax payable
< $250,000	Nil
$250,000 to < $600,000	$275 plus 0.2% of amount > $250,000
$600,000 to < $1,000,000	$975 plus 0.5% of amount > $600,000
$1,000,000 to < $1,800,000	$2975 plus 0.8% of amount > $1,000,000
$1,800,000 to < $3,000,000	$9375 plus 1.3% of amount > $1,800,000
$3,000,000 and over	$24,975 plus 2.25% of amount > $3,000,000

QLD — land tax rates

Total taxable value	Rate of tax
$0–$599,999	$0
$600,000–$999,999	$500 plus 1 cent for each $1 more than $600,000
$1,000,000–$2,999,999	$4,500 plus 1.65 cents for each $1 more than $1,000,000
$3,000,000–$4,999,999	$37,500 plus 1.25 cents for each $1 more than $3,000,000
$5,000,000 and over	$62,500 plus 1.75 cents for each $1 more than $5,000,000

SA — Land Tax Rates and Thresholds

Total Taxable Site Value	Amount of Tax
Does not exceeds $353,000	Nil
Exceeds $353,000 but not $647,000	$0.50 for every $100 or part of $100 above $353,000
Exceeds $647,000 but not $941,000	$1,470.00 plus $1.65 for every $100 or part of $100 above $647,000
Exceeds $941,000 but not $1,176,000	$6,321.00 plus $2.40 for every $100 or part of $100 above $941,000
Exceeds $1,176,000	$11,961.00 plus $3.70 for every $100 or part of $100 above $1,176,000

WA — Land Tax Rate

Aggregated Taxable Value of Land		Rate of Land Tax
	Not Exceeding	
$0	$300,000	Nil
$300,001	$420,000	Flat rate of $300
$420,000	$1,000,000	$300 + 0.25 cent for each $1 in excess of $420,000
$1,000,000	$1,800,000	$1,750 + 0.90 cent for each $1 in excess of $1,000,000
$1,800,000	$5,000,000	$8,950 + 1.80 cents for each $1 in excess of $1,800,000
$5,000,000	$11,000,000	$66,550 + 2.00 cents for each $1 in excess of $5,000,000
$11,000,000		$186,550 + 2.67 cents for each $1 in excess of $11,000,000

TAS - Rates of Land Tax (from 1 July 2010)

Total Land Value	Current Tax Scale
$0 - $24 999	Nil
$25 000 - $349 999	$50 plus 0.55% of value above $25 000
$350 000 and above	$1 837.50 plus 1.5% of value above $350 000

16

Business Asset Protection

Now that you know about trusts, it's worthunderstanding how these can be used in thebusiness world for asset protection.

It's a sad fact that certain industries and professionals are more susceptible to litigation than others. While we certainly recommend asset protection for every business *owner,* we don't recommend the following asset protection for every *business.* Professionals such as doctors, industries with employees on work sites and businesses that own considerable plant and equipment are examplesofbusinesses that should consider some form of asset protection.

As a note, before considering any asset protection one should have adequate insurance as a stop-gap.

For a business that has a tremendous amount of value in machinery, equipment or intellectual property, these items should be held separately from the trading entity.

Here's an example:

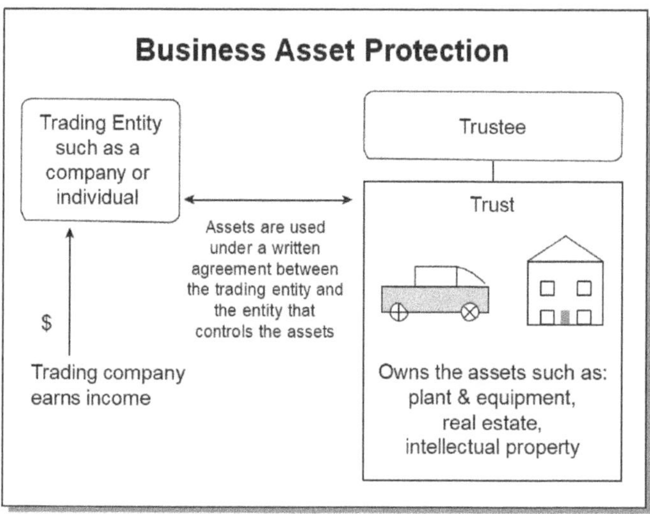

If the professional or business is sued by either an employee or a client, the assets are protected because they are owned by a separate entity and used under a license agreement.

In such a circumstance, all the business owner does is wind up the trading company, establish a new one and re-establish a new license agreement, like so.

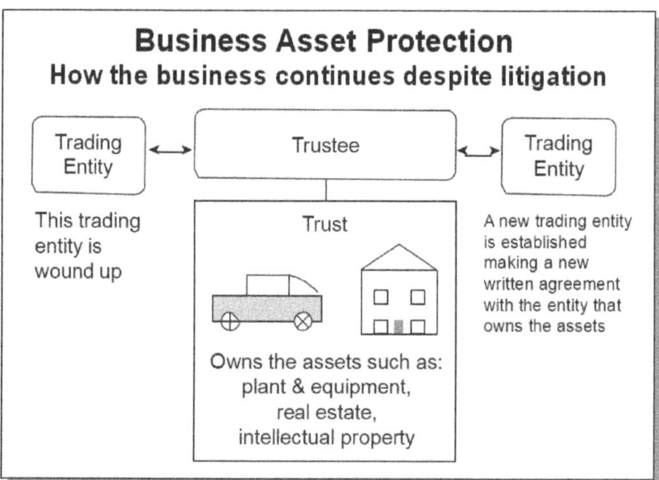

A useful analogy is that the business is like a tree, with the main trunk being the most important part. Tree branches may fall off from time to time but the tree trunk continues to grow. All effort and energy goes into keeping the tree growing and not allowing anything to harm it. So it is with a business or investment—keep it growing and protected.

As far as what type of trust should be used, you guessed it—that depends on your personal situation. The point to note is:

- ▶ **Business assets should be protected in a separate entity, especially in highly litigable industries.**

17

What Is the Best Business Structure for You?

This is an area that business owners often neglect, but it can have a significant impact on your net worth if you get this wrong upfront.

When entrepreneurs start a business, their thoughts are usually on cash flow, market positioning, financing, employees, work hours, risk and the like. They seldom look at what is the best business ownership structure to achieve these outcomes and longer-term wealth creation. Even fewer think of the cycles their business will travel through or the changes that are going to occur over time, both to the business and to themselves and their family.

When launching a business, consider what structure is best suited to it, now and in the future, and the reasons why. Business structure is something you need to address before you start opening bank accounts, signing leases,purchasing plant and equipment, employing staff andregistering any intellectual property. It should be step one.

At Chan & Naylor, we believe that you should always start with the end in mind. This means that when you're launching your business, you need to identify your long- term goals and needs. For instance, you may one day wish to protect the assets that you have built, you may require flexibility if your circumstances change, you might want to sell part or all of your business, or you may want to bring in new partners.

The structure that you use to set up your business will impact your abilities to make these decisions in the future. Business owners who neglect this risk having to pay tens of thousands of dollars or indeed much more if they find that they need to restructure somewhere down the track.

It makes good practical and business sense to separate your various assets into different structures, according to whether they are personal or business assets and, further, between depreciating and appreciating assets.

When you first set off on a new business venture, you don't want to assume that something will go wrong; but you do need to prepare and plan for the unforeseen. As well as that, you should in fact plan to be significantly successful. By setting up your ownership structure correctly, you minimise your exposure to risk so that if anything ever does go wrong, there is no impact on your personal assets or wealth. To change this later exposes you to potential additional expenses such as capital gains tax and stamp duty.

When operating your business, you should implement procedures and processes that limit your risks and exposure to litigation. You can achieve this by ensuring you act responsibly and within the laws, and also by taking out relevant insurances. Your final safety net is to run your business through an appropriate ownership structure. This way, if any unforeseen events occur, your other assets are not exposed to litigation or loss.

Essentially, what you're doing is creating a "safe harbour" for your wealth to ensure that the wealth stays within the family (intergenerational wealth), with an additional benefit of not exposing your wealth and assets to any sort of risk. As a side note, you should also be aware that the "goodwill" and intellectual property and trademarks you create in your business are valuable assets and must also be protected.

Beyond risk and asset protection, there are other important and practical reasons for using the most appropriate ownership structure for your business. These include:

1. Estate planning
2. Wealth creation
3. The impact income tax might have on your cash flow

4. Capital gains tax (CGT), particularly if you sell the business or introduce new partners (including family members)
5. An efficient and effective mechanism to pass assets on to the next generation
6. Flexibility

WHERE TO BEGIN

The main structures for owning and operating a business are loosely grouped into four categories:

1. Sole trader
2. Partnership
3. Company
4. Trust

There are advantages and disadvantages to all of the above, but the majority of business owners operate under options 3 or 4: a company or a trust. At Chan & Naylor we seldom recommend trading under options 1 and 2—as a sole trader or partnership—as these structures don't effectively manage or address estate planning, flexibility and asset protection concerns, and in the case of partnerships, expose both parties to the acts of the other party.

Sole trader is the simplest structure and is used by many business owners. Under this structure, all income (after deducting all business-related expenses) is taxed at the sole trader's personal marginal income tax rate. Capital gains on a sale of the business or its assets would go to the sole trader and the 50% CGT general discount rules would apply. Sole traders must apply for an Australian Business Number (ABN) and Tax File Number. As it is a simple structure, both the operating costs and the administrative requirements are minimal.

However, this structure provides no asset protection, and if anything goes wrong in the business, all personal assets are also exposed. All income and capital gains would be attributed to the sole trader and there is no flexibility on their distribution.

A similar situation exists with partnerships. This type of structure puts every partner at risk for the actions of each of the other partners. Therefore, the actions of Partner A can impact Partner B and his or her assets. There are some benefits to this structure; if you are a husband and wife team, for example, it allows for the income to be distributed as you wish, based on a fixed agreement. However, in most cases, the benefits of running your business as a partnership are faroutweighed by the potential risks. Note that there can be partnerships between individuals, companies and/or trusts but the underlying issue for most arrangements is that each party will be liable for the actions of the other party with whom they are in partnership.

For the remainder of this chapter we will focus our attention on company and trust ownership structures.

CONSIDERATIONS—GST AND PSI

Before contemplating starting a business, the issues of goods and services tax (GST) and personal services income (PSI) need to be considered.

All businesses, irrespective of structure, must register for an ABN. Although it isn't mandatory, we recommend that business owners also register their business name with the respective state government agency.

GOODS AND SERVICES TAX (GST)

In summary, GST is a 10% tax applied to the gross revenue invoiced, less any GST paid on the goods or services acquired to provide the sale that generated the gross sales revenue. You need to add 10% to your base selling price; this must be paid to the ATO (irrespective of whether you make a profit) less any GST you paid on your inputs. If your business activities will generate more than $75,000 gross income per financial year, then the business must register for GST. When reviewing your GST position, you need to become familiar with the following terms:

- **Registration**: You must register for GST if youcarry on an enterprise (business) and the revenue from your business activities exceeds $75,000 per financial year.

- **Taxable supply**: GST is payable on each sale. The supplier must be registered and operating an enterprise; and the supply must be for consideration and primarily in Australia. It must not be GST free or Input taxed.

- **Input tax credits (ITC)**: The GST paid by yourbusiness and claimed back on taxable supply sales.

- **Input taxed supplies**: The sale of goods and services where GST does not apply and the supplier cannot claim credits for any GST paid on their own acquisitions. Examples are financial services and residential property.

- **GST free**: No GST is payable on the purchase but the supplier is entitled to claim credits for the GST payable on its acquisition.

- **Tax invoice**: To be able to claim ITC, your acquisition must be supported by a tax invoice showing the supplier's ABN and price breakdown, identifying the GST component.

PERSONAL SERVICES INCOME (PSI)

PSI refers to any income generated by personal exertion. In other words, it is income that is mainly a reward for an individual's personal efforts or skills, and it must be attributed to them personally for tax purposes.

You qualify as a personal services business if any of the following applies to your situation:

1. You meet the results test:
   - Income is paid to achieve a specified result or outcome;
   - You provide the necessary tools and equipment (if required) to do the work; and
   - You are liable for rectifying defects in the work.

If, in a given income year, 75% or more of your personal services income meets all three conditions, you pass the results test for that year.

OR

2. Less than 80% of your personal serq1vices income in the financial year comes from each client, and you meet one of the other three personal services business tests (the unrelated clients test, employment test or business premises test).

OR

3. You obtain a determination from the Australian Tax Office confirming that you are a personal services business.

COMPANY OWNERSHIP STRUCTURE

The majority of businesses operate through a company. A company is a separate legal identity in the eyes of the law; therefore, it separates the business operations from the individual operators, providing a layer of asset protection. In limited circumstances, the directors of a company can be held personally liable for the actions of the company, such as if a company operated while insolvent, or the directors engaged in fraudulent acts.

A Proprietary Limited (Pty Ltd) company is only required to have one director and one shareholder. It is governed by the rules of the company, called the "Constitution". The tax rate of a company is a flat rate, which is currently 30% or 27.5% for small business turnover under $10m (current as of publication date; for the most up-to-date information check www.ato.gov.au).

All income and assets belong to the company. If you wish to withdraw funds from a company, you can do so by either paying a salary or via the payment of a dividend to the shareholders after you pay the appropriate tax.

If you own your business in a family company structure, this means that the company is owned by individuals. In this case, each individual holds an asset (shares in the company) and these assets would be available to creditors in the event of litigation. The loss of the shares could mean the loss of income and a valuable asset to the individuals.

Asset protection is not a normal benefit of a company structure, as a company only offers limited liability. This means that if the company is sued, only the assets within the company are available to creditors and normally shareholders are not required to fund any additional amounts. Directors, as previously explained, can be exposed under limited circumstances. If the shareholder is successfully sued they could lose their shares and therefore part of their wealth.

The following diagram sets out the most common basic ownership structure for a family company.

XYZ PTY LTD XYZ Pty Ltd operates business

Shareholders or Members

- Person A Dad—one ordinary share (being 50%)
- Person B Mum—one ordinary share (being 50%)

Office Holders

- Person A Dad, who works in the business—Director and Secretary
- Person B Director. This could be Mum, but we would not recommend this as she would be caught up in any litigation and, as a result, family assets such as your family home would be more at risk. (Maybe have Dad, who operates the business, as the only director.)

As a basic example, if $100 net profit was generated:

The company receives $100.

Tax is paid at the company rate of 27.5%, which is $27.50.

The remaining $72.50 profit is distributed to shareholders, with $36.25 going to Person A and $36.25 going to Person B. The split of dividends depends on the number of shareholders and their individual percentage ownership of ordinary shares.

Because the $72.50 was paid after XYZ Pty Ltd paidAustralian tax on all its earnings, the $72.50 dividend is said to be "fully franked".

As this example shows, from a cash-flow perspective, you are required to pay tax before you receive any money to do other things, such as invest.

The shareholders also receive the money in the form of a dividend, which can be "franked" (meaning tax has been paid at the company rate of 27.5%) or "unfranked" (meaning no tax has been paid).

Shareholders who receive unfranked dividends are required to pay the appropriate amount of tax according to their income tax bracket. However, if they receive a franked dividend, they will also receive a credit for the tax that has already been paid by the company. This can become complicated, so if you use this ownership structure, it's worthwhile discussing these matters with your accountant before the end of the financial year.

When choosing the best ownership structure for your business, it's worth taking into account your future plans in regards to selling the business.

Capital gains tax is a tax that is payable upon the sale of an income-producing asset, such as a business or a piece of real estate. Individuals are entitled to a 50% discount on the amount of CGT that is payable if they hold on to the asset for at least 12 months. A company, however, is not entitled to receive the 50% CGT discount.

If you sell your business the buyer will normally not want to purchase the shares as they will then take on any liabilities in the company. Buyers will want to buy the business, not your shares. Therefore the company sells the assets etc, including goodwill, and receives the cash. The capital profit is attributed to the company, which does not get the 50% CGT discount. The problem then arises as to how to access the funds. Unfortunately this normally means higher tax. The extraction of the funds is a complex matter, and prior to any sale you should consult your tax accountant.

There are many other complex issues associated with CGT and company structures, including the fact that it is relatively difficult to get the profits out of the company and into your hands without paying additional tax.

If a client decides to use a company to operate their business, we recommend the following structure:

XYZ PTY LTD XYZ Pty Ltd operates business

Shareholders or Members

Hybrid or Discretionary Trust—one ordinary share (being 100%)

As the trust is not a legal entity (refer to the section on trusts below), it will require a company to act as trustee. The shareholder and the office holders of a trustee company (additional company to XYZ Pty Ltd) could be individuals, as the value of a trustee company would be nil. Risk would be minimal but an individual is required as director.

Office Holders of XYZ Pty Ltd

Person A—Director and Secretary (being the person actually operating the business)

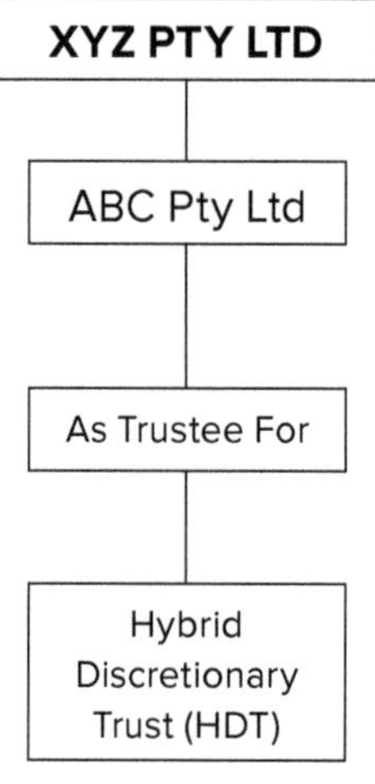

XYZ Pty Ltd operates business. Dad would be Director, and shares would be held by the trust.

Shareholders or Members

Hybrid Discretionary Trust (HDT)—two ordinary shares (being 100%)

The HDT would have an ABC Pty Ltd company as trustee and Mum and Dad would be the shareholders 50/50, with only Dad as Director.

After-tax profits would flow down from XYZ Pty Ltd to the HDT for distribution to any family members. If XYZ Pty Ltd had paid its full tax (currently 27.5%) then this would be used as franking credits in the hands of any family member who received a distribution from the trust.

In this structure, we have replaced the shareholder with a trust for the following reasons:

1. More flexibility when distributing dividends to trust beneficiaries, which allows for better management of tax planning but still using after-tax funds.
2. Better asset protection, as the shares of the company are held in the trust. In the event that the individuals are sued, they are not holding an asset in their own names.
3. More flexibility in relation to capital gains treatment when the business is sold.

When the business is sold, the trust (being the shareholder) will receive the profits, which can then be distributed to any beneficiary. Note that similar limitations apply to the trust shareholder as for the individual, in relation to the company distributing either dividends or capital on liquidation. There is still the issue that the company does not receive the 50% CGT discount as in the above section. The main advantage is that the shares are not owned by individuals but by a trust.

Whilst the company does not receive the 50% CGT discount, it pays 27.5% CGT on assets sold. However, if the business was held personally or in a trust which distributes the capital gains to the individual who is entitled to the 50% CGT discount, instead of paying 47%, he pays 23.5%. When compared to the company tax rate of 27.5%, it would appear that it's cheaper to hold it either individually or in a trust. The difference is that when an individual pays tax, the money is gone forever. When a company pays tax, it goes into a franking account where the tax can be claimed back later if a franked dividend is paid. Effectively you can draw dividend from the company tax free if your personal tax rate is the same as the company, and if less than the company you could even get a refund, or if your tax rate is more than the company, you could have a tax payable but only the portion above the company. Example: personal tax rate is 21% you would get a refund at 6.5% (27.5% less 21%). If your tax rate was 47% you would pay a top up tax of 19.5% (47% less 27.5%).

TRUST OWNERSHIP STRUCTURE

The main benefit of a trust structure is that it provides flexibility. Income can be distributed to the lower-income earner, assets can be protected and wealth can be passed on to the next generation with minimal fuss and little or no tax payable.

To be clear, a trust is not a legal entity; it is basically an agreement or promise. It is also a vessel that holds assets on behalf of beneficiaries.

Put simply, a trust is simply an agreement (trust deed) between a trustee (the legal owner) and beneficiaries (beneficial owners) that in the event of certain things happening, certain things will occur.

For example, the agreement might be that if the trust generates profits from business activities, then the trustee can distribute this profit to beneficiaries at its discretion, and each beneficiary will then pay the appropriate amount of tax according to their personal situation.

It is critical to understand that the trust owns the assets—not the beneficiaries or decision makers. Therefore, if these groups find themselves in litigation, the trust assets are not available to creditors.

Also, as it is the trust that is generating the income (subject to PSI rules), the trust cash flows can be distributed to beneficiaries in any proportion.

Trusts come in all shapes and sizes. The type of trust that is most suitable for you and your business depends on many factors, such as the type of asset or business, financing, income type, marriage status and susceptibility to being sued. Be wary of anyone who says, “Such-and- such trust will suit all situations”, because that is simply not true. Typical trust types include family, discretionary, unit, fixed, hybrid, Property Investors Trust (PIT) and superannuation.

A trust is a legal document (the deed) that explains how assets are to be treated. Therefore, the rules identified within the trust deed formalise what sort of trust it is, not the label used to describe it. The trust is only as good as the rules that have been written in the deed.

POSITIONS IN A TRUST

A trust is essentially an agreement by which a person or company agrees to hold assets for the benefit of another. The one who holds the assets is called the trustee; those who benefit are called beneficiaries.

There are four main positions in a trust structure:

1. **Trustee**—the decision maker
2. **Beneficiary or principal**—the receiver of the benefits
3. **Appointer**—the person who decides who the trustee will be. Without doubt, this is the real position of power
4. **Settler**—the person who helps set up the trust. Note that once the trust is set up, the settler plays no further role. Typically the settler gives $10 to set up the trust. Not all trusts require a settler.

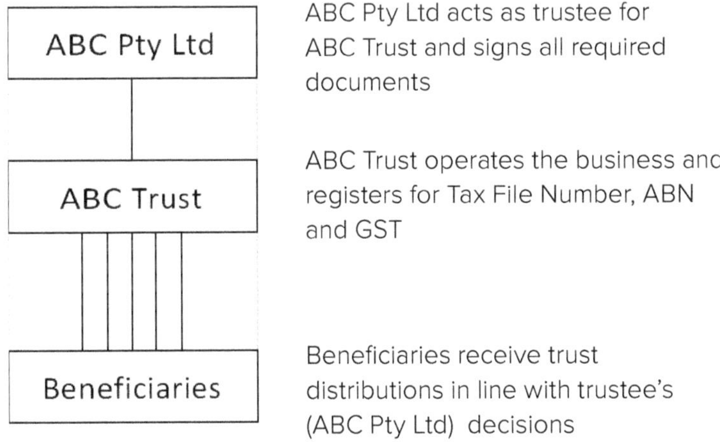

The trustee has legal control, which is legal title only. A person with legal control can buy and sell an asset but will never own or enjoy the benefits of ownership, such as income or usage. It is the trustee's name that appears on all legal documents, bank accounts, etc. As previously discussed, it would be recommended that only those family persons operating the business be directors.

The beneficiaries are not necessarily all mentioned in the trust deed. They have beneficial ownership (allowing a person to enjoy the benefits of ownership, including usage, income, profits, etc) and are entitled to the assets and profits of the trust. Normally people specifically named are the partners. The trust deed typically captures by category (such as children, parents etc) all relatives, companies and trusts associated with them and the spouses of those people.

THE BASIC FUNCTION OF A TRUST

The basic function of a trust is to separate control and ownership. The result is that asset protection is possible and profits can be distributed in the most efficient way.

When you establish a trust of your own, you have both legal control and beneficial ownership. Most people don't separate the roles; they think they're one and the same, but they're not.

For example, asset protection occurs because even though legal title is in the name of Joe Bloggs, Joe is trustee for a trust and therefore doesn't actually own the assets: they are held in trust for the beneficial owners. Hence nothing can be taken from Joe, because he doesn't legally own it.

Ownership plays a key factor in not just asset protection, but also in estate planning and within the tax system too. A star Player will own nothing and control everything!

There are many aspects of operating your business via a trust structure that you can use to your advantage.

Given the special nature of running a business and allowing a follow-through to the next generation while creating maximum estate planning and asset protection, Chan & Naylor has developed a specific trust for business called a Business Enterprise Trust (BET).

Our BET caters for the practical and commercial needs of running a business, and also allows you to grow and protect your assets from generation to generation. The BET covers the following:

1. It is capable of introducing new "owners", including but not limited to family.
2. It allows for changes to beneficiaries.

3. It is possible to easily change appointers and trustees.
4. Any distributions can be restricted to family lineage, ie no in-laws.
5. It lasts over a long period of time. Trusts normally cease after 80 years; the BET has no end date.
6. It allows the business's appreciating assets—such as business real property, goodwill, intellectual property, etc—to be owned outside of the business.
7. It easily allows for a distribution to another entity such as a trust where property, for example, is held. The benefit of this is that if the trust with the property is negatively geared then pre-tax money from the BET can be distributed (via family trust election) to the loss-making trust.

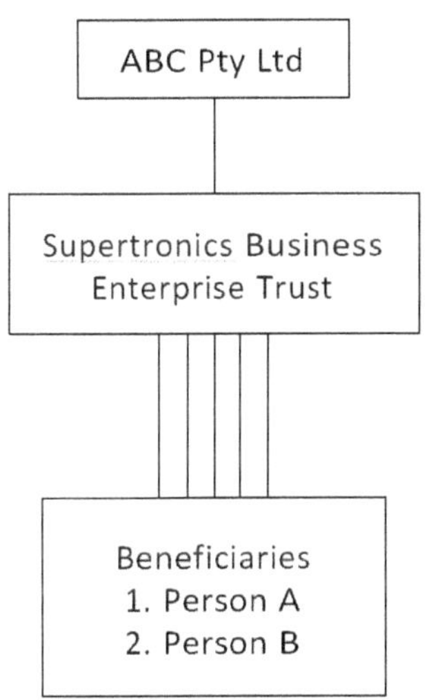

ABC Pty Ltd acts as trustee for ABC Trust and signs all required documents

Supertronics Business Enterprise Trust operates the electronics retail business and registers for its own Tax File Number, ABN and GST. It may also register Supertronics as a business name.

Beneficiaries receive trust distributions in line with trustee's (ABC Pty Ltd) decisions. Children, parents, other relatives, associated companies and trusts are also captured as beneficiaries without specifically naming them. It would NOT be advisable to specifically name others.

If the net profit (revenue less expenses) from this trust was $80,000, the distribution to beneficiaries could apply as follows (based on 2017/18 tax rates):

1. Person A: $39,168 (tax $5,059.96)
2. Person B: $39,168 (tax $5,059.96)

3. Remainder to the four minor children: $416 each (tax nil)

The total tax payable on $80,000 is $10,119.92, or just under 13%. The tax calculations were correct at the time of writing; from time to time you should check the ATO website (www.ato.gov.au) for the tax rates that apply as they are subject to change.

Note that trust distributions to minors are heavily taxed to discourage income splitting, minors can earn $416 each without tax. Income earned by minors through their personal exertions is taxed at adult tax rates.

Had the $80,000 been paid as dividends or partnership income to Person A and Person B, a total tax of just under $10,964 would have been payable, compared to approximately $10,119.92 via the trust (refer to ATO website for any updated tax rates). However if you have a child 18 or over who has not earned enough to reach their threshold it can be an advantage to distribute income to him/her.

Having said that, a trust should not be used solely to reduce tax, or Part IVA of the ATO's anti-avoidance rules would apply, and higher tax rates would be applicable. In this case, if Person A and B could demonstrate that a trust structure was used because they were concerned about asset protection, estate planning and a more efficient mechanism for wealth creation, then it is unlikely that the anti-avoidance legislation would apply.

As you can see, from a cash-flow perspective, with the BET the profits of the business flow to the beneficiaries before any tax is paid, which is a significant difference to the company structure—especially if you are an investor leveraging your assets via gearing.

The primary advantages of using a trust structure, and in particular the BET, are clear, as it allows for:

1. Distributions of business profits before tax
2. The ability to plan and manage the timing of tax payments
3. Flexibility
4. Estate planning
5. Asset protection

PROTECTING BUSINESS ASSETS

Whatever structure you decide to use to operate your business, consider separating the value or goodwill of the business from the trading entity itself. Many people, through no fault of their own, find themselves facing financial hardship, so if you are making a substantial investment in a business over many years, it makes sense to try and protect this in the event of unforeseen circumstances.

Investigate having a separate structure to hold assets such as equipment, goodwill, intellectual property, databases, brands or anything of significant value. This separate entity simply enters into a commercial agreement and licenses the right to use the assets, or leases the ability to use the equipment, back to the business.

The above may seem a little confusing, but it works. This structure will allow the most flexible opportunity for growth and dealing with unforeseen occurrences, while also benefiting you and your family by protecting the family assets and generating flexible distributions.

The starting point is the BET. The other structures can be added on as circumstances roll out; for instance, the Value Trust illustrated in this diagram will only be established if and when such assets are evident. For many businesses, the purchase of business premises and the creation of intellectual property may not eventuate from day one, but the BET allows for these "bolt ons" to be added if and when required.

The ideal ownership structure for you will depend on your business and your situation, but ideally you want a structure that allows the business to grow uninhibited as your needs change. As with anything involving complex legal and financial matters, you should always seek solid professional advice.

We recommend you see the Accountants at Chan & Naylor: www.chan-naylor.com.au.

18

Superannuation: A Taxed Savings Plan

I've never met a wealthy person who saved their way to financial freedom. Wealth is created by *action*. When the only method used is saving, then it's an inactive, fearful attempt at providing for the future.

You must certainly spend less than you make and it's prudent to keep a portion of your income aside— that is the basis of all sensible money management. But to rely totally on your savings for the future is a road to poverty.

As a nation we tend to spend everything we earn and then some, with credit cards or "buy now and pay later" interest-free purchases. In 1992 the government forced every working individual to save. They called it superannuation. It was the answer to a society that spent everything. But why didn't they *also* teach people about money and how to create wealth?

The purpose of superannuation is to provide money for you when you retire. So here you are at age 60 or 70 or whenever it is you retire and this is when you get the money they've been saving for you. How much will it be? Well, that depends on a few things. But we can tell you this—it would be more if it wasn't taxed. Did you know that your super money is taxed? Yes, your super contributions are taxed at 15%. So you will only ever see 85% of what is contributed. Furthermore, if your super makes a profit that too gets taxed at 15% for income and 10% for a capital gain.

And that is the government's plan for your retirement!

Force you to save and then tax it!

Superannuation is better than nothing but why should a solution for funding retirement be handicapped so much? Yet it is promoted that super is a good thing because you pay less tax if you put more of your salary into it. Why would you put more money into a fund over which you have little or no control and that you won't see untilyou're 60? Because you've been sold the idea that someone else knows more than you about what to do with *your* money. So what can you do about maximising your super?

Well, you can't eliminate the taxes but you can manage it yourself with a Self-Managed Super Fund (SMSF). A SMSF has many benefits and rewards but does require some participation on your part. To find out more about Self- Managed Super, read *How to Buy Property With Your Super Money* available online at www.chan-naylor.com.au

Depending on your age and how much you have set aside in your super, there are many benefits to operating it yourself, the least of which is being able to invest in property, choose shares or even choose managed funds.[32] A SMSF reduces management fees and provides investing flexibility and freedom—it is, after all, *your money.*

It fits with the Tax Factor:

►You own nothing and control everything.

Before making decisions about superannuation you should seek the advice of a licensed financial planner. To find out more visit our website:

www.chan-naylor.com.au

32 **managed funds:** an investment fund managed for a number of clients by a company, often involving a combination of fixed-interest and property investments at the discretion of the fund managers.

19

Maximising Your Tax Deductions and Reducing Your Tax

When it comes to tax, everything we've covered so far puts you way in front of the hard-working, salary-earning Australian. Understanding entities such as companies and trusts means you've joined the elite; learning about property and non-cash deductions alone can save you thousands. Yet all of this knowledge is totally useless unless you use it. Both this chapter and the next are dedicated to helping you grasp the fundamentals so that you can put to use the tools you've come to learn about. The first thing to know is:

WHAT IS A TAX DEDUCTION?

The ATO criteria and definition of a tax deduction is:

1. It must be spent.
2. It must be necessarily[33] incurred in earning your income.

A definition we use is:

- **A tax deduction is an expense that is related to your income.**

33 **necessarily:** inevitably, essentially.

The formula for calculating your net income follows easily from this definition and can be expressed as:

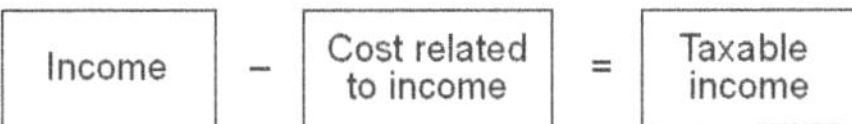

No matter how complex the system becomes with new taxes and different laws, fundamentally this basic formula applies: whenever you spend money to make money that's a tax deduction, but only if you were making the money first!

SELF-ASSESSMENT SYSTEM

As mentioned earlier, here in Australia we have a self- assessment tax system. You absolve your accountant of responsibility every time you sign a tax lodgement. It's true that the accountant is dependent upon you to provide the necessary information to calculate the tax deductions and profits. A trained professional accountant or tax agent uses their know-how to include all the deductions and work out your tax bill. Once all the work is done, in a complete role reversal, assignment of full responsibility and accuracy is then handed over to you. You give them the information, they do the work and it's up to you to decide if it's right!

This is the current tax system. You could liken it to a brilliant computer whose manufacturer boasts about its amazing ability to calculate massive figures at lightning speed or produce the most up-to-date reports at the press of a button. Imagine then you put this computer into the hands of an untrained person who can't tell the difference between the monitor and the keyboard and ask him to produce a report. And if the report is wrong he is in trouble. The outcome, of course, would be comical and even if he was trained on how to use the computer, no matter how good the computer was, it would only be as good as the information entered into it in the first place.

The point we're making is that you need to know what you can put into your tax return; and this knowledge extends beyond the input provided by your accountant. You know, accountants have a tough job (yes, this is a sympathy plea on behalf of accountants everywhere) staying abreast of the law while also acting in the best interests of their clients. It's a constant juggle between acting in the client's favour by pushing the boundaries and simultaneously remaining compliant. If you ever want a living example of being stuck between a rock and a hard place, then be an accountant for a day!

Nevertheless, no matter how proactive your accountant may or may not be, the end result is this:

- **The size of your tax deductions is directly related to your ability to know and track all your expenses.**

This factor is primary to having a "good accountant". Using our definition of a tax deduction, you can easily determine if an expense is a tax deduction or not. If you're unsure, then by all means get a second opinion. A proactive accountant is one who works with you to really maximise your deductions, but it is up to you to first make sure you've tracked and included all possible expenses. If you don't tell your accountant that you spent $100 on tolls or include it in your bookkeeping, how will it ever be deducted?

The simple act of seeing *how* an expense could legitimately be related to your income-producing activity is the key and it also, incidentally, gives you a great index as to the proactiveness of your accountant. Is he or she *willing* to see *how* an expense *can* be related or do they just dismiss the "tricky" ones without regard?

For example, if your job entailed a considerable amount of time working outdoors then safety sunglasses could be a related expense. But you'd have a tough time relating sunglasses to an office job!

Therefore, willingness to look outside the box is required by both you and your accountant.

The first step, however, is to record the sunglasses as an expense. If you're ever in doubt as to whether an item is an expense or not, include it in your bookkeeping and nut it out with your accountant at tax time. If you fail to record it in the first place then you've lost the opportunity to claim it altogether.

So part of being an investor or business owner is making that extra effort to record and claim all that you legitimately can. After all, you've worked for the money and by organising your paperwork you'll be able to keep that little bit extra in your back pocket!

THE FLOW OF MONEY

While the definition of a tax deduction is simplified to a cost relating to your income, there is still an area of confusion that we commonly witness. Understanding that the flow of money can affect the ability to claim an expense means that each and every transaction has a consequence.

In addition to the definition of a tax deduction is the Tax Factor:

- **Where the money flows determines the tax deductibility.**

Let's quiz you on this one.

If you own an investment property and borrow against the *investment property* to buy a *home* to live in, is the interest on the loan a tax deduction?

No. Why? Because the purpose of the loan was to buy a home, the money flowed to the home, which is not tax deductible.

Okay, next example: if you borrow money against your home to buy an investment property, is the interest tax deductible?

Yes—because the money is flowing towards the investment property.

Be sure to check out the real life examples in Part 3 where you'll see this scenario covered.

NEGATIVE GEARING—A COMMON SOURCE OF CONFUSION

People often think that a $5000 share trading course can be offset against their salary. This may be true for a stockbroker or financial planner but if you're a fireman or clerk, you've got no chance of proving any relationship between your salary and a share trading course.

Per our definition of a tax deduction, the expense has to be related to your income. This assumes that you've made money in that line of business. So the cost of a share trading course can be offset against income from share trading or other related activities—but you have to make an income to offset it against!

The reason for this confusion is, presumably, the negative gearing tax laws. Any loss on an investment property can be offset against personal income whether you are in the real estate business or not. A janitor, clerk, executive or tradesman can claim the loss of owning an investment property as a tax deduction against their income, whether salary or wage. This is allowed because the government has created a special ruling, but it only applies to investment property.

We have seen all too often where a misunderstanding of this fact has led people to spend money on courses or training in the belief that it will be offset against their current income. Unfortunately, this is not the case. You do have to be earning money directly related to the expense before you can claim against it. Also, beware of this trap when establishing a new business; expenses incurred prior to actually making an income in that business can only be classed as a capital expense. This means that the cost of set- up is not deductible against income; it can only be offset against a capital gain should you sell the business. This is often a cold, hard shock to some people who count on getting the initial set-up cost as an income tax deduction.

WHAT IF I GET AUDITED BY THE ATO?

There is a general principle which applies:

- **In Australian tax law, you are required to prove that you are innocent.**

This may sound a little rough but it's a fact. A tax audit is based on the fact that you must prove you have been doing your tax returns properly. The word "audit" in this sense means to examine or inspect carefully.

As you know, we have a self-assessment system, which means that *you* decide if it's a tax deduction. If, during an audit, the ATO says "No, this is not a tax deduction," you can ask for a private ruling or go to court and fight it or simply pay the tax on that deducted item, with possibly a little interest and perhaps a fine to go with it.

Many arguments about whether an item is a tax deduction or not end up in court; it's the Commissioner[34] against John Doe (an individual) or the Commissioner against a corporation. This in itself demonstrates the complexity (insanity) of our system. When a case is voted in favour of, say, John Doe (in other words, the Commissioner loses), this is then used as an example

34 **Commissioner:** a government administrator. In this book it refers specifically to the Commissioner of Taxation of the ATO.

to back up a particular tax deduction claim. *Commissioner v John Doe* becomes the validation of written law, as opposed to the law itself. The result is that no accountant is 100% confident that any method, scheme or tax deduction will hold up under ATO scrutiny unless it has been "tested" in court.

Therefore, the answer to the question, "What if I get audited?" is:

- **In the case of an audit—the decision is based on individual circumstances in relation to other similar historical cases.**

Basically, if someone has fought the battle before you then chances are it will be smooth sailing and you shouldn't have a problem. However, if you're making inroads into uncharted territory then it could go either way. In the worst case scenario you're made to pay tax, interest and fines which could extend as far back as your first recorded usage of the tax deduction.

This section of the book isn't meant to scare you; it is how the game is played and most people who stay well within the simple guidelines have no trouble and need not go to court, but it's worth knowing how the system works. While a proactive accountant is willing to see "how" items can be deductible, a good one will also advise you if your submitted tax deductions or methods are too aggressive.[35] This is how the loopholes are closed, by the way. When the Commissioner loses a case, new legislation is written to prevent such action taking place in the future. These new laws tend to take effect from a certain date, leaving the loophole open to those Players already in the game. But the loophole is now closed for new Players who, in the never-ending game of cat and mouse, must find other means and methods that fit within current legislation.

If you're curious to see the results of different cases, you can search through the case judgments on the ATO website (www.ato.gov.au). It makes for interesting reading if you want to go to sleep and can't!

---

35 **aggressive:** in the finance sense, characterised by a willingness to accept above-average risk in pursuit of above-average returns.

SUMMARY

Make sure you record all expenses that are related to your income and on that basis include as much as you can! The next chapter gives you the method with which to track your expenses.

TAX FACTORS

- **A tax deduction is an expense that is related to your income.**
- **The size of your tax deductions is directly related to your ability to know and track all your expenses.**
- **Ask yourself, "How can this expense be legitimately related to my income?"**
- **Remember, you must first earn money before you can claim a tax deduction against it!**
- **Where the money flows determines the tax deductibility.**
- **In Australian tax law you are required to prove that you are innocent.**
- **In the case of an audit—the decision is based on individual circumstances in relation to other similar historical cases.**

20

Bookkeeping and Tax Returns Made Easy

We never cease to be amazed at how vital the skill of administration is; it affects every sector of one's life. Administration is defined as the methods or techniques used in running a business. It comes from an old Latin word *administrare* which means to serve or *manage*.

Any time you're dealing with money, you're running a business. Whether you are an employee or an actual business owner or investor, you have a financial department in your life that requires someone to manage it. And guess what—that someone is you!

And as soon as you delve into the world of tax and start playing the game, you inevitably run into the task of administration. You have, in effect, a "business" to run and the skills of administration are required.

The basic skill is handling paperwork and tracking your income and expenses since, as mentioned in the previous chapter, you have to include an expense for it to be deducted. This is obvious, but the skill and discipline of tracking everything can be missing and the result can be costly.

Expense tracking can range from a disorganised shoe box of receipts to every detailed transaction entered into a sophisticated finance software program complete with Profit & Loss statements[36] and balance sheets.[37] The latter is not

36 **profit and loss statement:** a list of your income and expenses.

37 **balance sheet:** the list of your assets and liabilities. Used to calculate the net worth of a person or organisation (net worth = total assets — total liabilities). See net worth in the glossary.

necessary, but a shoe box isn't really top class administration. You need to aim somewhere in the middle, with accuracy, efficiency and honesty in mind.

The reality is, you must get your paperwork and finances organised in such a way that *all* your possible expenses are included. To do this, you must first know what kind of information is really needed by your accountant. The information falls into three simple categories.

1. INCOME

Whether you earn your money from a job, business, share trading or investing of any style, all your accountant needs to know is the answer to this question: How much money did you make? Once this amount is established, the next question is: How much of it is a capital gain?

A capital gain, as a reminder, is profit from an asset such as shares, property, business, etc. If it was bought and sold in less than 12 months then you lose your 50% CGT discount so, in effect, the capital gain is counted as income and taxed at your marginal rate.

Lastly, your accountant will need to know when you made the money. And, in some cases, when you bought and sold an item.

2. EXPENSES

What expenses did you incur in generating a) the capital gain and b) your income? With these figures, it is a simple process.

3. TAXABLE AMOUNT

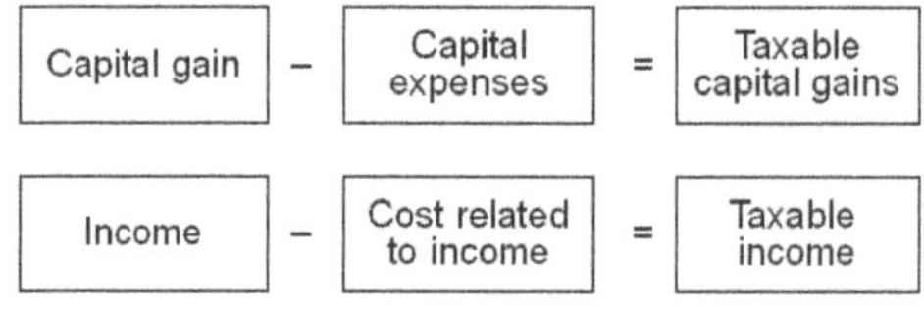

Let's use share trading as an example. Many people provide their accountant with a list of all the shares purchased over the financial year including how much they bought and sold them for. The first error in providing this kind of information is that not all accountants are share traders and therefore have no idea how to make sense out of this plethora of information. And even if your accountant is a competent trader, you're paying a lot of money for a professional to do a monkey's job.

As a share trader, all you need to do is work out the gross profit from each and every trade. Then add up all the brokerage,[38] stamp duty and all the other expenses that might have been incurred such as telephone calls, travel and overseas trips with your broker (only kidding!). You tell your accountant, "This is my profit and these are all my expenses, which add up to this." That's it—it's that simple!

SAVING TIME ON BOOKKEEPING

One of the best ways to track income and expenses is via your credit card or bank statement. Yes, you must keep all receipts and these are best filed in date order under specific categories for easy reference. But the best way to gather the necessary information for your tax return is from your statements.

Most statements these days include a brief description of where the money was spent; paying for fuel, for example, will show up with the name and location of the service station. Therefore, fuel expenses can easily be recognised and tallied.

Internet banking provides the facility of exporting statements that can be used in programs such as Microsoft® Excel® and others. This means that you can review your expenses and allocate them into categories on a regular basis. For example, you could export a one-month statement and separate transactions into categories such as income, fuel, stationery, vehicle and phone expenses and add these up as a total for the month. At the end of the financial year, you then have 12 months of totals for each category that you add up and submit to your accountant.

Remember that your accountant doesn't need to see the receipts and you don't have to prove the transaction. As long as you are honest and actually keep the receipts in case the ATO asks to see them, then that's fine.

For those of you who aren't familiar with the internet or computers, the cheque-book system works just as well. Just remember to write a clear explanation of what the expenses are and don't forget to review your bank

38 **brokerage:** the fee paid for the buying or selling or something. Normally associated with the buying and selling of shares.

statement to include bank fees and any other transactions you could possibly claim that come directly out of your account.

SEPARATE ACCOUNTS

To save time sifting through account statements, checking to see if each transaction was related to earning your income, it is sensible to have a separate account that you use for claimable expenses. The initial hassle of establishing another account far outweighs the time spent in later trying to separate the personal, non-claimable expenses.

TAX FACTOR

- **The basic information your accountant needs is:**

  a. **Total income.**

  b. **Total capital gain.**

  c. **Total expenses relating to both income and capital gain.**

  d. **The dates of the significant transactions.**

PART 3:

Real Life Examples

As you have most probably already grasped, there is no common solution regarding structuring as each individual's circumstances are different. However, now that you have an understanding of the basics, we thought we'd share with you some of the real life situations we've come across, how we handled them and the result.

We've taken examples from a broad spectrum of individuals; some are wealthy, others are on their way and some are just starting out on their financial journey. The names have been changed to protect the innocent! And while the situations are real, the stories themselves have been written to be interesting, educational and fun.

Enjoy!

List of Real Life Examples

"Rich Boy Loses Inheritance"

Jeff was worried about his son, Toby. He was a good kid and kept out of trouble but he liked to party and liked the girls!

When Toby turned 19, Jeff decided to pass on some of his wealth. Unfortunately, he wasn't very well advised and he gave a block of apartments directly to Toby, hoping that the boy would not waste or dwindle away his new fortune.

For Toby, all his Christmases came at once; the rent from the apartments was enough to buy fast cars and have plenty of fun without him ever having to work.

In short time, Toby found himself in love but his father was not so sure. The girl seemed nice enough but Toby had only recently met her as it seemed he had a different girl every week.

Jeff shared his concerns with his son, which unfortunately built up animosity between father and son. Toby thought his father was trying to control his life but all Jeff wanted to do was ensure Toby's financial future was protected. Toby's father relented and the wedding took place.

Within six months, Toby's carefree attitude about life faded. He was miserable. He and his new wife hardly talked; they now appeared to have very little in common. Through brief and infrequent phone calls Toby's father noticed his son's tone change and sensed that he was very unhappy.

One day, after much deliberation, Jeff decided to probe. "What's up, son? You seem miserable."

"Not much, Dad. Things are okay."

Smiling, Jeff said, "We all make mistakes now and then, and you know, what tends to eat us up more is the regret, not the mistakes."

There was a long pause and Toby finally spoke. "She wants to get a divorce and I keep trying to make it work."

"Do you want a divorce?" asked Jeff.

"Well … I don't know. I'm not happy the way things are but I feel like such a failure."

"No such thing as failure, son, only lessons," Jeff said wisely.

"But if I divorce her, she'll take half of the properties, or maybe even more."

Jeff nodded and said, "Happiness is more important than money and this lesson will serve you well."

Toby and his wife parted company. With a decent property portfolio at stake, the settlement ended up being fought out in court. The end result: Toby was left with 40% of his property portfolio, she took 60%. The properties had to be sold and after tax and legal fees, Toby's nest egg wasn't enough to live off any more. He invested it wisely with the help of his father and started his own business.

It's a sad tale, but it could have had a better ending if Jeff had done it a little differently. In the case of protecting assets passed on to children, here's how it can be done.

Instead of giving the properties to Toby, Jeff should have put them into a trust from the start and given the income to Toby via the trust. No matter who Toby married they would never be able to access the properties. This would only apply if the trust was set up prior to Toby getting married. Also, Jeff could have maintained control over the trust and only increased Toby's income when he proved himself worthy.

The point here is that control is the key factor. When passing on wealth to the next generation, it is worth ensuring that any potential mistakes your children make with money, choice of partners or business ventures won't jeopardise everything that you have "given" them, as long as you pass it on "protected".

"Land Tax Issue Drives Couple from Dream Home"

Cardiologists Dr John Martin and Dr Judy Stanford lived and worked in Sydney. After a long time searching, they found the house of their dreams. As they were in a high- risk occupation, they did not want their family home to be registered in their own names in case they were ever sued. They consulted a top law firm and were advised that they should buy their home in a Family Trust.

A Family Trust is a Discretionary Trust and is perfect for asset protection. One's principal place of residence is normally free of any capital gains tax and land tax if it's held in an individual's name. However, in NSW if a principal place of residence is held in a trust, it loses its capital gains tax-free status and is treated as an investment property, which means it is subject to land tax.

John and Judy settled happily into their new home, but when March arrived and their first land tax assessment turned up in the mail, they received a nasty shock. They had to pay $45,000.

Now this is an annual fee, so if they held the property for 10 years they would have paid $450,000 in land tax when normally they would have paid nothing. Naturally John and Judy were quite concerned.

They went and saw three top tax lawyers and four tax accountants in the city and after spending $35,000 in professional fees, they had a number of recommendations to consider, including advice to convert the Family Trust to a Fixed Trust. That way, they would at least be able to get a land tax threshold which would then save them around $6,000 in land tax. Various other "Band-aid" type solutions were offered, but all seemed to treat the "symptoms" rather than fixing the "problem".

After weighing up their options, John and Judy decided that the only solution was to sell their home, despite having paid just over $165,000 in stamp duty only six months earlier. They had already made contact with a real estate agent, with the intention of putting the property on the market, when a close friend urged them to go and see Chan & Naylor accountants before doing anything, as they were specialists in real estate.

Understandably, John and Judy were extremely sceptical—after all, as far as they were concerned, they'd left no stone unturned: they'd consulted the experts at the big end of town, sparing no expense, and none had come up with a good solution to their particular problem. When

they came into the meeting their first words were, "If our friend and colleague had not insisted that we come and see you, we wouldn't be here." Looking at their crossed arms and what could only be described as the cynical expressions on their faces, it was obvious they'd already decided the meeting was going to be a further waste of their time and money. "I don't know what you're going to tell us that we haven't already heard from seven top firms in the city," said John.

I have had many such meetings over the last 20 years, and the first thing I did was reassure them that if I could not help them after hearing their problem, there would be no charge for the meeting, and that I would know within 10 minutes.

As I predicted, within minutes the solution was obvious. "The answer is simple," I said. "As this is your home, the trust would simply grant you a 'life interest' for living in the property. In NSW the granting of a life interest attracts no stamp duty and if the life interest has been used for someone's home, then there is no land tax back in 2006." There was dead silence. The pair exchanged cynical frowns. Finally John said, "Are you sure about this? Is this legal? And if so why haven't any of the other legal and

accounting firms suggested this solution?"

"Well, John," I said. "I can't speak for the other firms but we specialise in this area and we see this on a regular basis."

Needless to say the arms unfolded, the faces lit up and the mood changed considerably.

Over the coming years, John and Judy referred many of their friends and colleagues to us and continued to spread the news that if you need solutions to problems concerning real estate you really should see Chan & Naylor first.

"Young Doctor Seeks Asset Protection"

John and Mary were moving up in the world. After spending several years hammering down the mortgage on their modest, two-bedroom apartment, they were finally at a stage where they could afford their dream home and it just so happened that they had recently found it. However, John and Mary wished to keep their apartment and rent it out. John was an up and coming doctor and was concerned about asset protection; Mary was expecting their first child and was concerned about possible litigation from tenants. Should a tenant sue them, then any assets that were in their names would be at risk to a successful lawsuit. For example if you have your home and two investment properties in your own name, then a litigant tenant or patient would have available to him all two investment properties, plus the home in a successful lawsuit.

Thankfully, before buying, they came to see their Chan & Naylor accountant!

"We want to keep the apartment and rent it out," John said, "but I want to protect the asset because I'm opening my own practice and don't want to lose it should I get sued."

"Who owns the apartment currently?" Ed asked. "We both do," replied John.

"Fifty-fifty?" asked Ed.

"Yes, is it possible to protect it?"

Ed, standing next to the whiteboard, looked at his captive audience of two, paused briefly and thought to himself, "So many people have come to me with this situation ... I should write a book about this stuff."

Ed drew a picture on the whiteboard and explained: "A Property Investor Trust™ (PIT™) should be established. John borrows the money, against the apartment, to buy the units in the PIT ™. The PIT™ then uses the money to buy the apartment (money flows towards investment and John owns 100%). John and Mary then use the money they have just received from the sale of the apartment to go out and buy their dream home.

"Although there may be stamp duty implications, there are no capital gain issues because the apartment was in their name and was their personal residence. Asset protection will have been achieved because the amount borrowed (to buy the units in the PIT™) is equal to the value of the units, hence John's net assets are nil.

"Additionally, as John is the only income earner, more will be saved on tax this way because he will receive 100% of the tax deductions from the investment property. And the new family home would be purchased in Mary's name."

After he got through explaining it all, Ed put down his marker and looked at his now happy audience.

"Where do we sign?" asked John.

John and Mary left the meeting promising to name their first born "Edward", even if it's a girl!

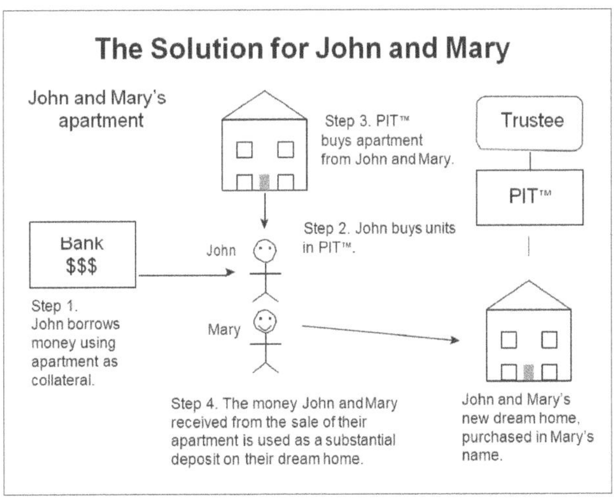

RESULT SUMMARY

No Asset Protection—Assets Owned by John and Mary

Structures:	None
Asset Value:	$450,000—apartment $65,000 mortgage $650,000—new home
Asset Ownership:	John 50% and Mary 50%
Income:	$120,000 John's salary $26,000 Mary's wage
Tax Deductions:	50% of the interest on $65,000 for John 50% of the interest on $65,000 for Mary

Ed's Solution

Structures:	PIT™
Asset Value:	$450,000—apartment $65,000 mortgage $650,000—new home
Asset Ownership:	PIT™, with all units owned by John.
Income:	$120,000 John's salary $26,000 Mary's wage
Tax Deductions:	100% of the interest on $450,000 for John (being an 80% loan on the apartment) and home value.
Establishment Cost:	$1500 plus stamp duty on sale (approx. $25,000)
Ongoing Fees:	$1000
Tax Saving:	Assuming 7% interest on the loan, John can claim $25,200 against his income, every year saving $7938 in tax (at 31.5% marginal rate)

PRE-RESTRUCTURE-TAX POSITION

NON-DEDUCTIBLE LOAN	DEDUCTIBLE LOAN	TOTAL LOAN
$ 650,000 Purchase price $ 25,000 Stamp Duty (approx) $ 1,500 Legals (approx) -------------------------------------		
$ 676,500	$65,000	$741,500

Assume interest rate 5.5%*$65,000 = $3,575 pa tax deductible

POST – RESTRUCTURE – TAX POSITION

John borrows $450,000 to buy $450,000 at $1 per unit in PIT™ and PIT™ buys apartment off John & Mary. They use the $450,000 cash to pay off loan of $65,000, leaving $385,000 cash to pay off their private mortgage of $676,500, which then leaves a private non-deductible debt of $291,500.

(Assuming Stamp Duty on sale of apartment to PIT™ was paid in cash – no loan required.)

NON-DEDUCTIBLE LOAN	DEDUCTIBLE LOAN	TOTAL LOAN
$ 291,500	$450,000	$741,500

Assume interest rate 5.5%*$450,000=$24,750 p.a. tax decutible.

Tax saved (Assume 39% tax rate) $9,652.50 p.a.

Tax saved over 20 year loan $193,050.

"Accountant Reported Missing as Lady Receives Four Years of Tax Deductions in One Fell Swoop!"

Maria Corleone was an astute property investor, with no less than 15 properties to her name worth almost $6 million. She came to us as a client and wanted her tax returns done. She had a feeling that her accountant, who she referred to as Joe Bloggs, wasn't doing all that he could. She was sharp and straight to the point, with no messing around. She was dangerous in an indescribable way; you got the idea that she was not the kind of lady you wanted to upset.

A review of her portfolio and past tax returns revealed that depreciation on her properties had never been claimed. Her previous accountant simply hadn't done it. Not in all the years she had owned the properties.

Before telling Maria this, we first worked out how much she could still claim. Knowing that you can go back a total of four years (now can only go back 2 years from 27/10/2016) and claim depreciation if it was not claimed, we sat down and did the figures. Armed with the good news, we called in Maria.

After the standard pleasantries, we explained to Maria that her previous accountant, Joe Bloggs, had failed to claim depreciation on her properties. As her voice echoed throughout the office and the unrepeatable profanities reverberated across the state of New South Wales, we calmly mentioned that there was some good news. Of course, she didn't hear us so we had to repeat it several times.

When we finally got through, we explained that although she'd missed out on the last 20 years of depreciation, she could claim the last four years (only can go back two years now).

Maria paused for a moment as she digested this and then with almost a hint of a smile asked, "How much?" Fumbling with our paperwork and smiling politely we found the figure. "You can claim about $50,000, giving you around $25,000 tax refund," we said, hoping for a smile.

We looked at her as our pulses raced. Did she hear us?

It was hard to tell. Then after some time she smiled! "Thank you, gentlemen," she said politely as she got up. "I'll be back in one week to sign the papers. Now I'm off to see my old accountant."

We scanned the obituaries for weeks but found no entry under Joe Bloggs.

"Structure Overkill: Distraught Young Woman Seeks Help ..."

Tina was a computer operator for a medium-sized firm. She earned $45,000 a year and was definitely a woman who knew what she wanted. Despite only being in her late twenties, she was in the process of buying two investment properties. Surprisingly, she'd already sought asset protection advice but unfortunately was ill-advised.

When Tina came to see us, she had two Discretionary Trusts (both with a different company as trustee) for each property. "Keep them separate," she was told, "for better asset protection." Although this holds some slight truth, it's a little over the top.

Here's what was wrong with this set-up:

1. Tina was not in a profession or industry prone to litigation and need not have taken such drastic measures. She was an employee and not a director of the company she worked for.
2. The Trusts had a Vesting date, which meant that sometime in the future it was going to trigger a capital gains tax and stamp duty problem for her children.
3. She had quarantined her negative gearing. This means that the losses from the property could NOT be offset against her income. The losses remained "in the trust". When we told her this, she broke down and cried.
4. Lastly, there was the cost of such an exercise: she had paid around $6000 to have the structures established. At the very least, one company could have been trustee of both trusts, saving

establishment fees of around $1200, not to mention the ongoing accounting fees.

Here's what we did:

Thankfully, and with some luck, she had only put an offer in for the properties and so they had not yet exchanged. Working quickly, we established a Property Investors Trust and she went ahead and purchased the properties using that structure. The benefits to Tina were:

1. Her assets were protected.
2. She was able to use her land tax concession and pay no land tax (not in NSW, this varies from state to state).
3. She was able to claim the negative gearing costs.
4. The Property Investors Trust™ has no Vesting date, thus ensuring she did not leave a problem for her children

Once we worked it all out, Tina managed a smile while wiping the tears from her eyes. She knew she'd wasted $6000 on the set-up of her initial structures, but was happy to be structured correctly now, and knew that despite that hiccup, with her properties now in a Property Investors Trust™, she would receive all of her money back in about 18 months.

Over the long term this means that if she holds on to the properties until she is 60 (she actually wants to pass them onto the next generation of little Tinas), her savings will be in excess of $429,000.

RESULT SUMMARY

Before

Structures:	Two Discretionary Trusts, with Corporate Trustees
Structure Costs:	$6000
Asset Value:	$600,000—twoproperties
Asset Ownership:	One property in each trust
Income:	$45,000 salary
Income Tax:	$6,747
Tax Deductions:	None

After

Structures:	Property Investor Trust™
Asset Value:	$600,000—twoproperties
Asset Ownership:	Property Investor Trust™
Income:	$45,000 salary
Income Tax:	$515
Establishment Cost:	$2,000
OngoingFees:	$2,000
Tax Saving Based on Income:	$6,800 saved in land tax every year plus negative gearing deductions (thisvaries from state tostate)
20-year Saving:	$429,000 in land tax, income tax and stamp duty.

Rent	$30,000
Expenses 20%	($6,000)
	$24,000
Depreciation	($10,000)
Interest $600k*7%	($42,000)
Losses	($28,000)
Wages	$45,000
Taxable income	$17,000
Tax free threshold	($6,000)
Taxable income	$11,000
Approx tax	$515

Getting Help with Your Next Step ...

At **Chan & Naylor**, we realise that becoming financially independent requires knowledge, experience and, every now and then, some guidance. Therefore, our purpose is:

> To teach every Australian how to become a real Player by providing applicable education, ethical advice and resources that increase investment returns and fast track their Road to Wealth.

Although we use the term "fast track", it is not a matter of getting rich quick; speed has more to do with sensible planning and the application of known principles and techniques. Our experience has shown that most overnight successes are not an overnight success at all; they're preceded by years of learning.

At Chan & Naylor, you'll learn how to get rich sensibly, first, by learning how to structure your investments and businesses. Second, through our ever- growing network of accounting offices and financiers, you'll have access to further education, investment advice and resources. To find out where to go and who to contact, visit www.chan-naylor.com.au or look in the back section of this book.

If you need a tax question answered, please email us via Contact Us section at www.chan-naylor.com.au/contact-us/

FEEDBACK: WE'RE HAPPY TO HEAR FROM OUR READERS

For us to provide education that is applicable to you and your future needs, we ask that you take the time to give us some feedback.

In a constantly changing world, it's important that we fully understand your different individual situations and the issues that may be preventing or slowing your progress on your way to wealth. Knowledge of topics such as tax, finance, money management and business, to name a few, are all vital to ensuring and speeding your progress towards financial independence. In this light, we invite you to tell us what other subjects you wish to learn more about and what difficulties you may be running into; email your feedback via www.chan-naylor.com.au website.

FINAL WORD

Remember that tax and tax reduction is second to making money. Don't get stuck on one side of the equation. Treat tax, money and life as a game and that way, despite any ups and downs, you will have fun. And isn't that what we are here for after all ...?

The Street-smart Factors of Legal Tax Reduction

1. You are not the only one who doesn't know **all** the tax laws—nobody does.

2. You are either a Player or a Pawn in the game of tax.

3. A Player gets paid first.

4. Legal tax reduction ... It's up to you!

5. You never invest or willingly lose money just to get a tax deduction. Never.

6. To play the game of tax you need to be either a business owner or an investor (or both).

7. The term ROI is an acronym for two phrases:

    - Return **Of** Investment is measured in the **time** it takes to return your investment.

    - Return **On** Investment is measured in a dollar amount or percentage.

8. The tools of the tax game consist of structures, the ROI concept and future planning.

9. The Player always follows the Investor Sequence™.

10. There is no such thing as "one-size-fits-all" when it comes to structures. Each person's circumstances are different and need assessing before embarking on the use of structures.

11. Nobody owns a trust—it is controlled, not owned.

12. You own nothing and control everything.

13. The best time to set up asset protection is before you invest.

14. When property ownership is shared your tax deductions are also shared.

15. Investor ownership must be decided before purchase.

16. Asset protection and your investment strategy are deciding factors of property ownership.

17. A Depreciation Schedule should always be used for investment properties built after September 1985.

18. Any legitimate expense associated with your investment falls into one of two categories:

    - Claimed as an income expense (100% deductible or depreciated over time).
    - Claimed as a capital expense when the investment is sold.

19. Property ownership affects land tax.

20. Business assets should be protected in a separate entity, especially in highly litigable industries.

21. A tax deduction is an expense that is related to your income.

22. The size of your tax deduction is directly related to your ability to know and track all your expenses and your knowledge of tax laws.

23. Ask yourself: "How can this expense be legitimately related to my income?"

24. Remember, you must first earn money before you can claim a tax deduction against it!

25. Where the money flows determines the tax deductibility.

26. In Australian tax law, you are required to prove that you are innocent.

27. In the case of an audit—the decision is based on individual circumstances in relation to other similar historical cases.

28. The basic information your accountant needs is:

    - Total income.
    - Total capital gain.
    - Total expenses relating to both income and capital gain.
    - The dates of the significant transactions.

29. Focus on the right side of the equation—making money is more important than tax.

Frequently Asked Questions

Q: I have heard of the term "leverage". What is it and can it be applied to both share investing and property investing? And which is better—shares or property? And why?

A: Leveraging is increasing your assets in ways that involve borrowing money. It can be a much faster way to generate wealth than saving and paying down your debt. By acquiring more assets, even if you don't own them outright, you have a larger asset base working for you, which in effect creates greater and faster wealth. But leveraging could also increase the size of your losses, unless you build in precautions and safeguards.

To determine which is more effective—investing in shares or investing in property—let's look at the leverage ability of both asset classes. With shares you can generally borrow up to 50% loan value ratio (LVR) of the asset itself. This means that if you have $100,000 to invest you can borrow a further $100,000 to achieve a share portfolio of $200,000. Therefore you now have $200,000 working for you instead of $100,000.

Property, on the other hand, gives you the ability to borrow up to an LVR of 80% of the property itself. This means that if you had $100,000 cash you could borrow $400,000 to purchase a property worth $500,000. Therefore you would now have $500,000 working for you instead of $200,000 as in the above example with shares.

It's fair to say that some banks will lend more than 50% LVR against a share portfolio but this is rare; most banks will only lend up to 50% LVR. Additionally, if the shares fall in value most share loans require that you top them up (margin call), which is not normally the case with a property loan.

Some people may say that shares give you a better return on your investment, even though the base is smaller.

However, in the example above the share portfolio of $200,000 would need to return an average of 35% pa (excluding franking credits) for you to end up with the same amount of money that would be returned from a $500,000 property earning around 14% pa (capital growth of 10% per annum and rental yield of 4% pa). Remember, we started off with the same deposit of $100,000.

If you were able to achieve a 35% pa return over the longer term, then it would be better to leave your money where it is.

Q: My partner and I currently rent a place together but are considering investing in a property, with the view to maybe moving into it later on. As we're not yet married, what's the best way to structure ownership so that we're both protected if we ever do break up?

A: There are several things to consider. The first is the tax implications. The property should be bought in the name of the person who pays the larger amount of tax in order to get the best refund from the ATO. However, if that person is in an occupation that attracts litigation (for example a medical specialist or someone in business), then it is not advisable to buy the property in their name in case they are sued over a professional matter, which could then result in losing the asset in a law suit. (If asset protection is a concern, then it's best to purchase the property in a "Property Investors Trust" in which case the property is not held in the name of the at-risk individual but in the name of the Property Investors Trust.)

The person will still be able to claim the tax deduction against their wages/salary since they borrow the money from the bank to buy the units in the Property Investors Trust and the trust buys the property. The rental, net of expenses, is paid to the unit holder, who then claims the interest on the loan as a tax deduction. The individual achieves asset protection because a creditor cannot force the unit holder to sell their units to redeem the equity (assuming there is equity). The units can only be redeemed by the trustee, and in this case the trusteeship would be jointly held between the partners (married or de facto).

If you happen to separate later, divide the proceeds from the sale according to the amount you each contributed to the property. To enable this to happen cleanly and accurately, you should keep detailed records of the funds you each put towards the purchase of the property, including repairs/ improvements.

Asset splits and tax implications—whether between husband and wife or de facto partners—are treated completely differently to each other. If there are children involved in a separation, everything gets a lot more complicated as the Family Law Court simply looks at one thing only—the welfare of the children. The assets are generally divided in such a way as to cause minimal disruption to the children's lives. In the case of entities such as trusts and companies, the Family Law Courts do not take account of what name the assets are held in and will group all the family's assets together and divide them as they see fit, with the aim of ensuring as little disruption to the children as possible. For example, the primary caretaker is generally assigned the family home in order that the children stay in the same school and maintain their friendships. The primary earner continues to make a contribution towards the care and maintenance of their children and the primary caretaker until the children reach an independent age.

Q: I am in the process of purchasing my first investment property. Could you clarify the situation in regards to money spent on improvements and/or repairs to the property in the first 12 months and how this expenditure is treated tax-wise?

A: If you spend money on an investment property immediately after you purchase it, the ATO will not allow you to claim that whole amount as a tax deduction because they would argue that you bought the property at a discounted purchase price, given the need for the renovations. So the cost of the renovations is treated as part of the purchase price (to which it is added, in order to reflect what the property should have been worth). However, you can claim the depreciation on the property as a tax deduction over a period of years.

If the house had been tenanted for quite a while and the property needs repairs due to wear and tear from the tenant, then the cost of the repairs required to bring the property back to its original condition is fully tax deductible.

If you undertake renovations that improve the original condition of the house, this is considered as an improvement, not a repair. Hence you cannot claim the cost of this improvement as a full tax deduction; however, you can capitalise it and claim the depreciation over several years.

Q: I would like to buy an investment property with two good friends and we're thinking of setting up a joint venture (JV) arrangement. Can you please advise on the best way to establish a JV trust? What should I know before I commit?

A: First of all I will state the obvious: buying property with friends can be fraught with danger. Having said that, the main thing to consider is how you can access your money.

Some of the issues are as follows. What if someone is contributing more money (deposit etc) or spending more time on the project than the others— how do they get a better return? How are major repairs paid for? What about future renovations?

What is the exit strategy and how will the property be valued? Can you refinance? How will funds be distributed and in what proportions? Will loans be joint and severable or severable only?

We often see situations where one party wants to exit and the other doesn't, which then raises the question: are profits distributed differently if someone exits outside of agreed terms? Also, be aware that buying in your individual names would trigger stamp duty and capital gains tax.

If you buy in a trust then you avoid stamp duty (in some states). Buying in a trust has land tax implications, especially in NSW, and depending on your objectives (buy and hold versus trade), different trusts need to be contemplated.

The above list is nowhere near exhaustive; it is just a sample of some of the issues for you to consider. When purchasing together with others, either individually or in a trust, we would recommend you seek legal advice and enter into a formal and detailed written agreement that sets out the terms and conditions, including the roles and responsibilities of each party, and incorporates an exit strategy.

Q: We're currently living in our own home, or principal place of residence (PPOR), and bought an investment property (IP) in January this year. We've leased out the IP for the past six months and are now thinking about demolishing it and building a new home, which would become our new PPOR. If we do this, we would also sell our current PPOR. If we decide to sell that improved property down the track, say maybe in five years, what would be the capital gains tax (CGT) liability? Can you please explain how CGT is calculated?

A: There are a few CGT rules applicable here:

1. An individual can only nominate one PPOR at any particular point of time, unless they are in the situation of moving from the old PPOR to the new PPOR. In that case, both houses can be treated as their PPOR and will be exempt from CGT for up to six months, subject to the old PPOR meeting a few conditions.

2. The investment property can be nominated as your PPOR from the time the property is vacated for the purpose of building the new PPOR. The old PPOR then loses its CGT exemption for the same period of time.

3. In the case of the rental property which then becomes your PPOR and is later sold, the CGT is calculated pro rata between the time you first bought it to the time you nominated it as your PPOR to when you eventually sell it.

Based on the above, let's use some real figures to illustrate your CGT choices.

Let's assume you bought the investment property for $450,000 (including stamp duty and legal costs) in January 2010.

You rented out the property until October 2010, at which time you started the improvements. These cost $350,000 and are finished in April 2011.

You move into the house in April 2011. The old PPOR is then sold in June 2011.

In April 2016—five years later—the new PPOR is sold for $920,000.

Option 1

You nominate the new house to be the PPOR from October 2010 (as per point 2 above). When sold in April 2016, the CGT on the new PPOR will be:

[$920,000 sale proceeds – ($450,000 + $350,000) property cost] x 9 months rental period = $14,400 gain. Six years and three months ownership period. The $14,400 gain will also be eligible to a further 50% CGT discount.

On the other hand, the old PPOR loses PPOR status from October 2010 but is entitled to six months' exemption (October 2010 – April 2011). Hence the old PPOR is subject to CGT for the period April 2011 to June 2011. The capital gain will be the sale proceed less market value at the time the property loses PPOR exemption in April 2011.

Option 2

You nominate the new house to be the PPOR from April 2011. When sold in April 2016, the CGT on the new PPOR will be:

[$920,000 sale proceeds – ($450,000 + $350,000) property cost] x 15 months rental period = $24,000 gain. Six years and three months ownership period.

Again the $24,000 gain will be eligible to a further 50% CGT discount.

Under this scenario the old PPOR is completely free of CGT from April 2011–June 2011, which is covered by the six-month exemption per point 1 above.

Choosing between the two options is largely dependent on the actual gain made from the sale of the old PPOR and the projected sale price for the new PPOR.

Q: I work for a large multinational engineering company and my entire division has just been made redundant, myself included, so I am using the opportunity to start my own engineering consultancy. My financial plan is to use the income generated by the engineering consultancy to generate the cash I need to purchase property, and ensure that it is positively geared. Since positively geared property is hard to find these days, I am planning to choose properties that are as close as possible to being positively geared, and then pay the principal down enough to effectively "force"-positive gear them. The engineering company is set up as a "pty ltd" company and has been in operation for approximately two years. I want to purchase the property in a trust, mainly for asset protection reasons. My accountant advises me against this because of capital gains tax disadvantages. However, I am not concerned by this since my financial strategy isn't based on making capital gains, but rather generating passive income.

My questions are:

(1) How do I move the income generated by the engineering consultancy into the trust? Am I able to simply operate the business from the trust and direct the income there?

(2) If I operate the business from the trust, does this still provide me with appropriate asset protection? Or does this expose the trust to being sued and potentially losing all the assets?

A: I'll start by answering your second question. It's not a good idea to operate the business from the same trust that owns the property because if someone sued the trust over a matter to do with your consultancy work, potentially you could lose the property in the subsequent legal fight.

The appropriate trust for the property would be a "Property Investors Trust" (PIT), which is a different type of trust to the one you should use for the consultancy business. The trust for the consultancy should be a Family Trust. This gives you the flexibility to distribute income from the Family Trust to the PIT to "soak up" any negative gearing in the PIT. It may be negative on paper, due to depreciation on the property.

In regard to your first question, the options are:

Appoint the existing company as trustee for a Family Trust and drive consultancy income into this Family Trust. Income from the Family Trust can be distributed anywhere. Buy your investment property in a PIT. This will give you asset protection because your passive assets are kept separate from your business, which is a higher-risk asset. You should never keep higher-risk assets in the same trust as your lower-risk passive assets. They should always be kept in separate trusts.

Leave the consultancy business in the existing company and continue to pay yourself a salary from this company. Set up a PIT for the investment property; you can then take out a loan in your name to buy units in the PIT. This will allow you to claim the interest on the loan as a tax deduction against your salary. This will give you asset protection because the property is held in a separate trust to that of your business.

Your accountant is quite incorrect to state that you should not have the property in a trust because of capital gains tax (CGT). A trust would give you a lot of flexibility with CGT.

It's best to see an accountant from Chan & Naylor to work through the finer details. For example, unlike other trusts a PIT has no vesting date; it is specifically set up for properties. A vesting date means the trust will vest its assets after a certain period of time and disappear. When this happens, CGT and stamp duty need to be paid. This will not happen if the property is held in a PIT.

Q: I am an overseas investor from Malaysia and have invested in two properties in Melbourne. As I do not reside in Australia and I am not an Australian resident yet, I assume I am not able to claim any of my properties in Australia as PPOR. As such, is it correct that upon disposing of my properties in future, there will be CGT liability for capital gains, even though I do not rent out the properties, ie no rental income? For the case above, what tax rate do I use to compute CGT? If I do have rental income in Australia, is the tax rate used to compute CGT similar to the tax rate used to compute rental income tax?

A: There will be CGT to pay when you dispose of your properties. As a non-resident you cannot claim the main resident tax exemption. If you owned the properties for more than 12 months, you are entitled to use the 50% general CGT discount on the capital gains. (CGT discount not available for non-residents after 08/05/2012). You are then taxed on the remaining 50% at normal tax rates but do not get the benefit of the threshold tax-free amount.

Therefore the tax rate from $0–$87k is 32.5% and increases through various levels to a maximum of 45% on amounts over $180k.

The tax rates are the same for rental income. If the properties were available and were rented, then any costs which you could not claim as a non-resident—ie negative gearing—could be included as costs to reduce any capital gain on sale. As a non- resident no Medicare levy applies.

As an example, let's say the property cost you $460,000 to purchase and you paid stamp duty of $14,500, legal costs of $2000, water rates and council rates of $3560 over the three years of ownership plus some repairs of $1200. This gives you a cost base of $481,260. If you sell the property for $650,000, then the capital gain used to calculate your capital gains tax is $168,740 after deducting your cost base.

However, you may have paid a real estate agent $12,000 in commission to sell the property and another $1000 in conveyancing costs, which will reduce your capital gain by another $13,000, thus leaving you with a capital gain of $155,740.

Capital gains tax is calculated at the same rate as income tax, but please note that the tax rates change every year. If you are a non-resident for the full year, the following rates apply for the 2017–2018 tax year:

Individual Tax rates 2017–18

Taxable income	Tax on this income
$0 – $87,000	32.5c for each $1
$87,001 – $180,000	$28,275 plus 37c for each $1 over $87,000
$180,001 and over	$62,685 plus 45c for each $1 over $180,000

Q: I operate my business through a company, the shares of which my wife and I own. We own several investment properties and our home is also in our names. Recently a friend of mine who is in business and has a similar company structure to ours was sued by one of his customers (creditor). He was forced to sell his home to pay the debts and also lost his business to the creditor. Can you explain why his home was taken when he is operating his business through a company which is a separate entity from himself? Surely this separation should have protected him from losing his house. Also, what can we do to protect our assets and avoid this happening to us?

A: Many accountants suggest that their clients should run their business through a company because the company tax rate is a flat 30% (or 27.5% for small business turnover under $10m). Also, because the company separates the business activities from their personal assets, if the business is sued then the personal assets such as the family home are protected. So far so good, except that frequently the husband and wife will own the company shares in their own names, will both be directors of the company and will purchase their home and any other investment properties in their own names.

The problem then arises that as a director of your own company, you can be sued along with your company. Therefore, if the law suit is successful then anything you hold in your name will be at risk.

For example, if the home is in the director's name, then that can be taken. Any other assets, such as investment properties and other investments in the director's name, can also be taken. Even the shares in the company which are held in the directors' names can be taken.

Some clients argue that the company share is a $2 share and therefore they can only lose $2.

However, after an evaluation is carried out, their business may be worth, say, $1 million. Thus the share has effectively increased from a value of $2 to $1 million. Hence there is now an extra million dollars in assets for the creditor to pursue.

These are very common problems when ccountants set up their clients' business structures. Needless to say we do not set up business structures this way. In the above question, the reason why your friend lost his house and his business was because he was a director of his company and, as a director, any assets in his name are exposed to creditors, including his home and the shares in his company. It appears that the creditor was successful in obtaining a judgement against the director, and the value of the judgement must have equalled the value of his home and his shares in the company. Thus he had to hand over his home and his shares in his own business to the creditor.

If an individual insists on operating their business through a trading company then at the very least the shares of the trading company should be held by a Family Trust, not in their personal name.

A better way for an individual to own a business is to separate the operating entity which deals with the public and hires the staff from the entity that owns the goodwill of the business. Thus an "Operating Trust" should be set up which is licensed the rights to use the goodwill from the "Goodwill Trust". This ensures that should the "Operating Trust" get in trouble, the goodwill and assets of the business, which are held in another entity called the "Goodwill Trust", are protected from any litigation. The owners could simply wind up the "Operating Trust" and start again by forming a "New Operating Trust".

In your case, the way to amend the situation is to change the company's constitution to allow the issuing of a Discretionary Share which entitles the shareholder to a dividend. A discretionary dividend could be paid to the value of the assets of the company, including goodwill; this would result in reducing the value of the assets of the company to nil. At this stage change the shareholders to a Family Trust and the problem is solved. You should then use an Equity Bank Trust to strip the equity from your home and investment properties, thereby providing them with protection.

Q: When is the right time to set up a trust for my property portfolio? Should I do this as soon as I start investing or after purchasing the first, second, third etc property?

A: Everybody's circumstances are different. For every 10 clients we see, about six of them will need a trust of some description.

For example, if you are in an occupation which attracts a lot of litigation, such as a surgeon, then it would be wise to set up a trust immediately for asset protection. You would not want any assets in your own name.

If you have one or two properties and you have reached your land tax threshold, then you may want to use a trust because in some states this gives you a new land tax threshold.

This would save you around $6000 a year in land tax in most but not all states of Australia.

However, if you are in NSW, it is better not to use a trust to purchase your first few properties because you will lose your land tax threshold, which you would generally be entitled to if you purchased in your own name. If you required asset protection then we would use an Equity Bank Trust to enable you to benefit from both a land tax threshold and asset protection in NSW.

So as you can see, the right time to set up a trust depends on your circumstances.

Q: I am interested in establishing a Self-Managed Superannuation Fund. Is there a minimum amount I need to have before I can set one up? Also, is there a minimum loan that I can take out?

A: There is no minimum amount required to set up a Self-Managed Superannuation Fund (SMSF).

However, it is often said that an SMSF should not have less than $150,000 to $250,000. To understand why, you need to look at the set-up expenses and the ongoing costs of maintaining the SMSF.

All SMSFs require a compulsory annual audit and lodgment of tax returns. The cost of these can vary from $1500 per annum to substantially more, depending on the work required.

For example, if the SMSF has $100,000 in Funds Under Management (FUM) and the annual maintenance cost is $1500, this equates to 1.5% of the asset balance of the fund.

Compare this with an industry fund, where charges are on average around 2% of Assets Under Management, although they can vary from 1–5%. As a benchmark, 2% of $75,000 is $1500. In other words, if you have around $75,000 in FUM, it will cost you approximately the same whether you use a SMSF or an industry fund. If you had less than

$75,000, then it would cost you more to run a SMSF because the costs are based on the amount of time it takes to prepare the tax return and financial accounts and this cost is generally the same whatever the amount of FUM.

If you had $1 million in an industry fund the fees to manage this fund would be $10,000 to $20,000 (at an average cost of 1%-2%). However, if you had $1 million in a SMSF you would only need to pay for the time taken to prepare the tax return and financial accounts. Therefore, if the assets consist of a single property this may only be $1500, or around $4000 if the SMSF trades securities and it takes more time to record all the transactions.

For anything above $100,000 FUM it would certainly be significantly less costly to run an SMSF. A super fund with $2 million FUM would cost on average $3500 to run as an SMSF as opposed to

$20,000 (1% fee) charged under an industry fund.

A SMSF cannot directly borrow unless it is through a Bare Trust structure. There is no minimum legal fund size for borrowing; the consideration is the lender's loan to value ratio requirements.

Note: Very large amounts in Super may be charged less than 1% in fees.

Q: Is it possible to use a Self-Managed Superannuation Fund to borrow money and buy property? What are the benefits of doing this?

A: The government has recently made changes to the way Self-Managed Superannuation Funds (SMSFs) can invest their money. In the past SMSFs were not permitted to borrow money and this meant they were unable to leverage except in certain circumstances (where they were able to leverage into shares through warrants).

On 24 September 2007 the laws were changed so that SMSFs are now able to borrow and invest in certain permissible assets such as property.

This is a very exciting opportunity for investors as, after receiving appropriate advice from a licensed Financial Planner, a person can roll over their existing superannuation from an industry fund or retail fund into their own SMSF. Then, through a similar warrant product (Bare Trust and a SMSF Limited Recourse Loan), they can borrow additional funds from a bank and buy property, thus instantly increasing their superannuation asset base.

Under Super Choice law, most employees can now opt to commence an SMSF, roll over their employer sponsored fund into their own SMSF and use the funds as a 20% deposit on their next superannuation property investment.

Note — The banks will require different loan-to-value ratios and can change from year to year or bank to bank.

The Super Guarantee (SG) contributions that their employer makes (ie 9.5% of the employee's salary) can be directed to the employee's own SMSF and, in conjunction with the rental income, can be used to fund the loan costs. The employee can also salary sacrifice (up to $25,000 p.a.—note that these figures are inclusive of any SG contributions to help with the repayment of the loan).

The exciting thing about this strategy is that once you reach 60, the SMSF can be converted into a pension fund and all income, such as rental and any capital gain on the sale of the property, is entirely tax free.

If the property was held outside of the SMSF (as in normal circumstances) and you wanted to pay down the loan amount, you would first need to pay up to 47% of your income in tax (depending on your tax rate), leaving a net of 53% to pay off the principal of the loan.

However, if the property was held within the SMSF environment, then after paying the contribution tax of 15%, you are left with 85% of your income to pay off the principal of the loan. This would naturally allow you to pay down the loan much faster.

In other words, when either your employer makes a superannuation contribution of 9.5% on your behalf and puts this towards your SMSF or you salary sacrifice part of your salary into your SMSF, you need to pay a contribution tax of 15%. That leaves you with 85% which can be used to pay down your loan principal. (Note: those who earn $250,000 p.a. will pay an additional 15% tax)

In some circumstances, if the property is negatively geared the depreciation on the property creates a paper tax deduction which can be used to offset the 15% contribution tax. In this case you end up with no tax liability and the full 100% of your contributions can be used to pay off the loan principal.

If you compare this strategy with holding the same property outside of superannuation, you would need to pay full CGT at 47% (23.5% tax with a 50% exemption if held for more than 12 months (assuming the highest marginal tax rate)) and the rental income would also attract tax at 47%.

Many clients consider that their super funds are not working very hard for them because in the past they were unable to use leveraging. However, with the changes to the current rules people can now work their superannuation funds much harder.

One word of caution: Bare Trusts (also known as warrants) only allow one property per trust and do not permit the release of the increased equity in that one property. So people who are in accumulation mode rather than retirement mode, and who want to purchase further properties, can either establish another Bare trust or see an advisor such as Chan & Naylor, who may recommend other solutions.

(Warning: This is not a financial or investment advice and you must seek the services of a Financial Planner before doing anything with a SMSF)

Q: My sister-in-law wants to sell an investment property that she bought through her Self- Managed Superannuation Fund (SMSF), and my husband and I are considering buying it. Are there any legal and tax issues we should be aware of?

A: The relevant legislation prohibits your SMSF from purchasing a residential property from a family member or associated and related party. There is no restriction on the reverse, so you can buy from the SMSF.

To help reduce concerns about the SMSF failing the sole purpose test, we recommend that the SMSF gets a written valuation from an independent registered valuer to establish the market price at which to sell the property to you.

The SMSF will need to pay capital gains tax (CGT) at 10% (nil if it was a pre-CGT purchase, ie the purchase was made before 20 Sept 1985) if the property was held for more than 12 months or normal tax at 15% if it was held for less than 12 months. You will also need to pay stamp duty on the purchase.

You will also potentially have a land tax liability, depending on the land value and other property you already own (excluding the family home).

Carefully consider the type of structure you use to buy the property— ie individual name/s or trust— as part of your estate planning and asset protection requirements, and take into account how interest will be treated for tax purposes if you are using debt to help finance the purchase.

Q: I currently own an investment property, which is tenanted. However, I want to develop the site with a couple of townhouses to be sold once completed. At the moment I'm able to offset (negatively gear) the investment property income against interest charges on the loan and other taxable expenses. What is the ruling once the property is no longer tenanted? While in the process of developing the site, how do I account for the mortgage interest (holding costs)? Is this then included as a capital cost of the development or is it an irrecoverable expense that can no longer be used as a tax deduction due to the fact that the property isn't producing income?

A: Whether or not expenses, including interest on your loan, are deductible comes back to your original intention. Namely, if your intention was to hold the properties as investment properties after the development is complete, then the interest is fully tax deductible throughout the construction period.

However, if your intention is to sell the properties once they are complete, then the interest throughout the construction period would need to be capitalised (ie added to the cost of the building, thus increasing the cost base of the development). When the properties are sold, this increased cost base reduces the profits and thus reduces the tax payable.

The tax on profits would be at the owner's marginal tax rates with no capital gains tax (CGT) discount.

You need to consider how you treat the land at the time when you begin to develop, as two different options are available, which may allow some of the profits to be treated as a capital gain with the 50% general discount as opposed to normal income which is taxed at marginal tax rates.

You will also need to address the issue of GST, because if you are intending to hold on to the properties and rent them out then the GST is payable on the building costs and there are no provisions that enable you to claim them back. However, if you are intending to sell the properties then you can claim back the GST on the construction costs but you will need to account and pay GST when the properties are sold.

There are significant decisions which need to be made before you commence the development, which, depending on your choices, will result in quite different tax outcomes.

Q: Should I buy my own home or should I continue to rent and put my money in an investment property?

A: The answer depends on whether you are asking the question from a financial point of view or from a lifestyle point of view.

Let's answer this question from both perspectives.

From a financial point of view it's better to live in the smallest and least expensive home and have all your money invested in assets that generate you both a capital gain and a rental income. Generally, you may get a 5–10% capital gain on property plus a possible rental income of 4–5%, averaged over a 10-year period.

So you will potentially receive 9%–15% per annum total return over the longer term.

Of course, when it comes to the home you own and live in, you miss out on rental income and only get a capital gain. Therefore the more expensive the home, the more rental income you will be forfeiting by living there. Over a lifetime this amount can be quite substantial.

For example, 4% of a $200,000 home is $8000 rental per annum that you forgo, but if the home is worth $2,000,000 you will lose $80,000 rent per annum.

However, the more expensive the home, the lower the rent return percentage. In other words, a property worth over $2,000,000 may only give you 2% net rental return. So in this example you may only receive rental of $40,000 per annum should you own an investment property worth $2,000,000.

This basically shows that it is cheaper to rent a luxury home than it is to own the luxury home.

Additionally, the loan you take out to buy your own home is generally a principal and interest loan, which means you are paying the loan down over a 30-year period and the interest repayments are not tax deductible. Plus the monthly repayments are generally higher on a principal and interest loan than on an interest only loan, which you would use to buy a rental property.

Whether you should own your own home or rent your home depends on what value you place on lifestyle versus wealth accumulation.

As stated before, if you place financial security/ risk above all else, then you should buy the lowest value home, pay it off early and when you are financially ready, invest in property. This would, however, not be the best wealth creation strategy because it's too conservative and too slow.

Remember, your own home only delivers you capital gain, whereas an investment property achieves both capital gain and rent return. So it makes sense to increase the asset class that brings you the greatest total return.

However, if lifestyle is just as important to you as financial security, then it may be better to rent your own home. This is because the rental you pay is generally less than a home loan repayment, which includes interest and principal. This is especially true when it comes to properties that are in the higher end price bracket.

However, if you are renting you should then buy an investment property at a higher value or, at the very minimum, at an equivalent value to the house you live in, and rent it out to a tenant. This allows you to be a player in the property market.

If the house you buy is rented out then the interest on the loan is tax deductible and after tax refunds are taken into account, the monthly payments will not be very great.

Hence, the combined monthly payments for both the investment property (after tenant's rent and tax refund) and the rent on your own home is generally less than the monthly interest and principal loan repayments you would need to pay for owning your own home.

In this way you will generally have a better lifestyle (ie, quality of home to personally live in) than if you were trying to pay off your home. At the same time you have an investment property that

is earning you around 5% - 10% capital gain and a rent return of around 2–4% per annum.

However, the final decision will depend on the individual, because some people feel much more secure owning a median priced home that they pay down and eventually own outright.

Others prefer a quality lifestyle above all else and rent an expensive home, while at the same time purchasing an investment property that allows them to take advantage of receiving both a capital gain and rent return, along with all the tax benefits.

The property market has doubled in value every 7 to 15 years for the last few decades and it's essential that you have some of your hard earned cash invested in this sector.

The above is just a general overview and the actual numbers will vary from person to person due to individual tax rates and interest rates on their loans.

Glossary

ABN Australian Business Number. All businesses must have this to be able to claim their GST expenses.

Aggressive In the finance sense, characterised by a willingness to accept above-average risk in pursuit of above-average returns.

Aggressive tax planning Aggressive methods of avoiding tax, which usually end up being exposed and rejected by the ATO. The penalty for those involved in such schemes can range from mere fines to a jail term. For more information on aggressive tax planning, the reader is advised to visit www.chan-naylor.com.au

Appreciation An increase in price or value.

APRA Australian Prudential Regulatory Authority; the prudential regulator of the Australian financial services industry. It oversees banks, credit unions, building societies, general insurance and reinsurance companies, life insurance companies, friendly societies and most members of the superannuation industry. APRA is funded largely by the industries that it supervises and was established on 1 July 1998. APRA currently supervises institutions holding approximately $2 trillion in assets for 20 million Australian

	depositors, policy holders and superannuation fund members.
Asset	A standard dictionary describes an asset as a possession, a thing of value. In the investing world an asset is something that increases your wealth, either by cash flow or capital gain.
ATO	Australian Taxation Office is the main revenue collection agency and is part of the Treasurer's portfolio. Its role is to design and manage systems that fund services for Australians.
Baby boomers	Those born after the Second World War, between the late 1940s and 1960s. This group makes up a large percentage of the population.
Balance sheet	The list of your assets and liabilities. Used to calculate the net worth of a person or organisation (net worth = total assets – total liabilities). See net worth in this glossary.
Beneficial ownership	Allowing a person to enjoy the benefits of ownership (including usage, income, profits, etc) even though legal title is in another name.
Beneficiary	The person who is entitled to the assets and income of a trust.
Brokerage	The fee paid for the buying or selling or something. Normally associated with the buying and selling of shares.
Capital gain	The value an asset increases by. If a house is purchased for $100,000 and is re-valued at $140,000 it has a capital gain of $40,000.
Cash flow	Movement of money received and spent; the pattern of income and expenses.
Capital gains tax	Capital gains tax is the tax imposed on an asset that has increased in value and is sold.

Commissioner	A government administrator. In this book it refers specifically to the Commissioner of Taxation of the ATO.
Company	A legal entity that is recognised by the ATO and therefore has its own tax and legal laws, which differ from those laws imposed on individuals.
Compliance	The work performed by an accountant to ensure you have followed the laws in regards to taxation. Literally means to submit.
Compounding	Adding to the original amount, making it larger.
Conveyancing	Transferring of the legal title of the property.
Corporation	Another name for a company.
Cross collateralisation	Where the collateral (security) of a single loan is guaranteed by more than one asset (usually a house).
Deciding date	A coined phrase for the beginning of the land tax year. The owner of the property at midnight on the Deciding Date is responsible for paying the land tax for the next year.
Deed	A signed document that outlines the terms of an agreement.
Depreciation	A decrease in price or value.
Director	The role in a company where the person is responsible for the direction and performance of the company. A company can have many directors.
Dividends	Profits of a company that are distributed to its shareholders; usually paid quarterly.
Due diligence	The process of checking and double- checking that an investment or a company is worth what the owner or seller says it is. It involves analysis of the profit and loss, balance sheet and cash flow statements. Often conducted by qualified accountants, although every investor needs to

	understand this process and realise all investing requires due diligence.
Entity	A separate structure such as a trust or company.
Exponentially	Rapidly increasing (as in size or extent) in an extreme manner.
Fire sale	Sale of assets at very low prices, typically when the seller faces bankruptcy.
Fittings	Furnishings; items that are added that could be removed. Example: lights or curtain rails.
Fixtures	In real estate, a piece of the property that is permanently attached. The fixture is considered a part of the property if it shares the same useful life as the rest of the property. Example: kitchen cupboards.
Fringe benefit	An incidental advantage; a benefit provided by an employer to supplement an employee's income (such as a company car or living away from home allowance).
Fringe benefit tax (FBT)	The tax paid on a fringe benefit.
Fundamental	The foundation, the basic requirements.
Gross	The full amount of profit or salary not including taxes, fees and other expenses.
Income tax	Tax paid on income. For an individual it is a progressively increasing amount. For a company it is fixed.
Incur	Make oneself subject to; bring upon oneself; become liable to.
Index	A number or ratio derived from a series of observed facts; can reveal relative changes as a function of time: a method of measuring. For example, the index of the stock market is used to determine the overall trend of the market on a daily, weekly or even yearly basis.

Indexed for inflation	This means the dollar figure is adjusted for inflation.
Inflation	The name given to the change in the value of money. Inflation of 5% per year means $1.00 is worth only $0.95 at the end of the first year, and only $0.90 after two years. You need to always take into account inflation when choosing an investment vehicle because it helps you determine if your money is going backwards. An economy with 5% inflation requires investments to return at least 6% because at 5% your money is neutral, and anything less is going backwards.
Interest only	A type of loan where your repayments only cover the interest.
Land tax	A tax on property imposed by states or territories; usually based on the estimated value of the property. See Office of State Revenue in this glossary for the state websites.
Land tax threshold	The amount of land that can be held free of land tax. It differs from state to state.
Legal control	Legal title only. A person with legal control can buy and sell an asset but will never own or enjoy the benefits of ownership (such as income or usage).
Litigable	Giving cause for a lawsuit: able to be pursued in court.
Macro	The bigger picture. (The global economy is a macro outlook compared to the Australian economy.)
Managed fund	An investment fund managed for a number of clients by a company, often involving a combination of fixed- interest and property investments at the discretion of the fund managers.

Marginal rate	The increasing tax rate paid on income as it rises. See Income Tax Rates Table in Chapter 5.
Member	The person entitled to the assets contained in a superannuation fund upon retirement.
Micro	The small picture. (Your personal micro financial situation compared to the nation's financial situation.)
Mortgage	A loan from the bank usually used to purchase a house. *Mort* is an Old French word meaning dead, and *gage*, also Old French, means a pledge—so, put another way, the word mortgage means a pledge until death!
Necessarily	Inevitably, essentially.
Net or Nett	The amount remaining after all deductions (taxes, fees and all other expenses).
Net worth	The different between your assets and liabilities equals your net worth. (Net worth = total assets – total liabilities.)
Office of State Revenue	A department of state government that administers the state taxation, and collects revenue, outstanding fines and penalties. See below for a list of the websites for each office:
NSW	www.osr.nsw.gov.au VIC www.sro.vic.gov.au QLD www.osr.qld.gov.au SA www.revenuesa.sa.gov.au WA www.osr.wa.gov.au TAS www.treasury.tas.gov.au ACT www.revenue.act.gov.au
Onus	A duty or responsibility; burden.
Pawn	A person who is affected by the constant changes in the tax law and does nothing about it.

P&I Principal and Interest. A type of loan where your repayment pays the interest and only a little bit of the actual loan amount.

P&L Abbreviation for Profit and Loss statement.

Personal guarantee The permission for a financial institution to claim your personal assets and income should the entity which borrowed the money (such as a trust or company) find itself unable to pay the loan.

Plant The equipment and machinery necessary for carrying on a business. For the property investor it relates to such things as dishwashers, ovens, etc.

Player A person who understands that tax is a game, knows the fundamentals of the game and continues to learn more as the rules of the game change.

Profit & Loss statement A list of your income and expenses.

Proprietary Limited Proprietary is relating to an owner or ownership. Proprietary Limited is a type of company whose ownership is limited to a certain amount of shares and shareholders; commonly abbreviated to "Pty Ltd". A company that has no restrictions on ownership is normally listed on the stock exchange, where its shares can be purchased by anyone; this is call a Limited type company and will have the abbreviation "Ltd" after its name.

Prudential Cautious, careful and considerate.

Quarantined Kept separate from something else by force; isolated.

Returns The income arising from assets such as property or shares.

ROI Return On Investment is the amount of money your investment makes. This can be expressed as

	a dollar amount or a percentage. ROI also means Return Of Investment—an investor always wants to know when they will get their money back. The combination of both the Return Of and On your Investment must be assessed before investing.
ROI gross	The Return On Investment before taxes, fees and expenses.
ROI net	The Return On Investment after taxes, fees and expenses—what you really made!
Ruling	Decision by authority: an official or binding decision, such as one made by a court or judge.
Savvy	Having a sophisticated understanding, well informed.
Scheme	Relates to aggressive methods of avoiding tax which usually end up being exposed and rejected by the ATO. The penalty for those involved in such schemes can range from fines to a jail term.
Shareholder	A person who owns a share, or a portion, of a company.
SMSF	Self-Managed Superannuation Fund. Where you are the trustee and one of the members.
Stamp duty	A duty (or tax) applied to some legal documents, especially on transfer of ownership. A stamp is fixed to a document to show that the duty has been paid and the transfer is valid.
Super contribution	The money paid into your superannuation by either you or your employer.
Tax	The charge against a citizen's person or property or activity for the support of the government.
Tax deductible	Able to be claimed against income.

Tax-free threshold	The amount of tax-free money that can be earned in a single year. (See Income Tax Rates Table in Chapter 5.)
Tax variation form	A form that a person can complete that allows their employer to reduce the amount of tax withheld from their wage or salary, thus increasing their take- home pay.
Tax return	The process of calculating your taxable income and submitting it to the government.
TFN	Tax File Number—a unique number that assists the government in monitoring and reconciling personal income and taxes.
Third party mortgage	When a loan is guaranteed by someone else's assets, rather than the assets of the person taking out the loan.
Threshold	A level or point at which something would happen or cease to happen.
Thwarts	Hinders or prevents (the efforts, plans or desires) of.
Trust	A trust is basically an agreement or promise to hold assets. The basic function of a trust is to separate control and ownership and, as a result, a trust provides asset protection and income distribution flexibility.
Trustee	The person with legal control who is trusted with the assets and decisions related to a trust or super fund.
221D	The old name for a Tax Variation Form, which is a form that a person can complete that allows their employer to reduce the amount of tax withheld from their wage or salary, thus increasing their take-home pay.
Yield	The income from an asset.

Player's To-do List

1.

2.

3.

4.

5.

6.

7.

8.

9.

10.

11.

12. --

13. --

14. --

15. --

16. --

17. --

18. --

19. --

20. --

21. --

22. --

23. --

24. --

25. --

26. --

27. --

28. --

29. --

30. --

Caring for your business & family from generation to generation.

Chan & Naylor is a national accounting group ranked in BRW's Top 100 Accountancy Firms in Australia. Established over twenty years ago by Edward Chan and David Naylor, Chan & Naylor was named BRW's fastest-growing accounting practice for three years running — in 2007, 2008 and 2013. We have offices in most major cities — including Melbourne, Sydney, Perth and Brisbane.

The secret of our success is a commitment to service, knowledge and meeting our clients' needs. We are recognised for our cutting-edge and innovative approaches to finding affordable solutions to our clients' challenges.

At Chan & Naylor, you can count on our knowledge in the following areas: tax strategies; small business; property investing; buying property using your self-managed superannuation fund; accounting services; and leading-edge strategies around asset protection and wealth creation — particularly via property investing, estate planning and tax planning.

Chan & Naylor have become one of the country's premier specialist accountants in the area of structuring, and within the firm we have nurtured an expertise that rivals — and even surpasses — some of the largest accountancy firms in Australia. Even partners of the largest accountancy and law firms come to us for their own personal accountancy needs. We prepare tax returns for over 6,000 clients.

Chan & Naylor is the model firm studied by thousands of students when undertaking their CPA studies from the Australian Society of Certified Practising Accountants and students completing their MBA at Queensland University.

Our motto is "To help our clients increase and protect their net worth from generation to generation".

Contact us now!

Tax-Information registration:

A **FREE 1**5–minute Question and Answer service is provided by Chan&Naylor.

To register your question please go to www.chan-naylor.com.au/contact-us/

Call us to make an appointment to discuss your tax and accounting requirements or call your local Chan & Naylor office direct. Details are on our website.

www.ingramcontent.com/pod-product-compliance
Ingram Content Group UK Ltd.
Pitfield, Milton Keynes, MK11 3LW, UK
UKHW012217240726
13966UKWH00003B/816

9 780648 258308